This belongs to: _____

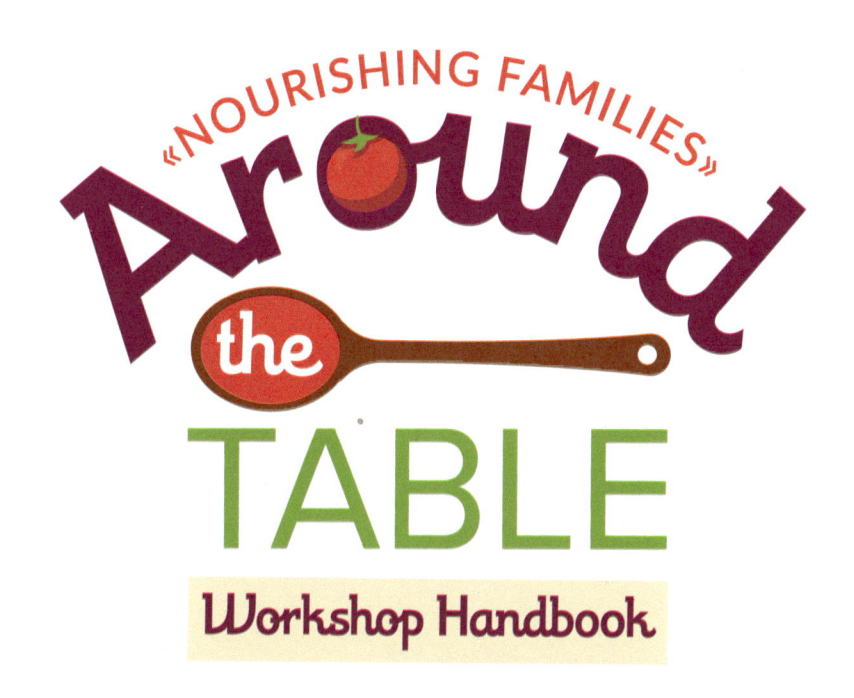

"NOURISHING FAMILIES"
Around the Table

Workshop Handbook

FAMILY & CONSUMER SCIENCES
UT EXTENSION
INSTITUTE OF AGRICULTURE
THE UNIVERSITY OF TENNESSEE

This material was adapted from and funded by USDA's Supplemental Nutrition Assistance Program (SNAP) under an agreement with the State of Tennessee.

This institution is an equal opportunity provider.

Programs in agriculture and natural resources, 4-H youth development, family and consumer sciences, and resource development. University of Tennessee Institute of Agriculture, U.S. Department of Agriculture and county governments cooperating.

UT Extension provides equal opportunities in programs and employment.

CalFresh HEALTHY LIVING | Leah's PANTRY

Copyright © 2020 Leah's Pantry (leahspantry.org).

Founded in 2006, Leah's Pantry has expanded from providing innovative nutrition education programming for low-income populations in San Francisco to a statewide organization that works with public and private partners. In addition to our grassroots work, we work throughout California to conduct nutrition educator training, manage the EatFresh.org website, and provide a comprehensive training and capacity building program for charitable food pantries. We are the first nutrition organization in the country to adopt a trauma-informed approach.

All rights reserved. No part of this publication may be reproduced, distributed, or transmitted in any form or by any means, outside of the Partnership Agreement between Leah's Pantry and partner organizations using *Around the Table* curriculum.

California's CalFresh Healthy Living, with funding from the United States Department of Agriculture's Supplemental Nutrition Assistance Program – USDA SNAP, helped produced this material. These institutions are equal opportunity providers and employers. For important nutrition information, visit www.CalFreshHealthyLiving.org.

Printed by Amazon KDP in the United States of America. Some images sourced from Unsplash and Adobe Stock.

v.10192020   ISBN: 9798322639695

Welcome to Around the Table: Nourishing Families

What does it mean to be nourished and to nourish my family? How does stress impact my ability to be healthy and what can I do about it? How can I find simple ways to practice good nutrition and feed my family delicious meals? How do I support my family's emotional and physical vitality through food?

Feeding ourselves and our families can be both enjoyable and challenging. You are invited to gather with a community of other parents and caregivers to explore how to nourish our families' bodies and spirits.

Enjoy!

Contents

■ Workshop Activities 7
- Conversation Questions: Exploring Our Food Histories 8
- T-Rex in Traffic 9
- Stress and Your Body 11
- Conversation Questions: Feeding Our Families 12
- Food, Mood, and Energy 13
- Toxic Stress: Awareness and Resilience 15
- Conversation Questions: Creating a Loving Food Environment 17
- Food Prep: It's a Family Affair 18
- Conversation Questions: Nourishment Away From Home 19
- Outsmart the Grocery Store 20
- Don't Label Me! 21
- Canned, Boxed, and Bagged 22
- Conversation Questions: Nourishment in Our Communities 23
- My Family Coat of Arms 24

■ Recipes and Menu Planning 25
- Index of Family Friendly Recipes 26
- Meal Planner & Budget Tracker 29
- Baby Tomato Bites 32
- Banana Sushi 33
- Black Bean and Vegetable Tostada 34
- Chicken Caesar Pasta Salad 35
- Chicken Lettuce Wraps 36
- Chicken Soft Tacos 37
- Corn and Black Bean Salad 38
- Egg Burritos 39
- Fish Tacos 40
- Fresh Veggies and Dip 41
- Fruit Crisp 42
- Fudgy Fruit 43
- Green Smoothie 44
- Korean-Style Vegetable Pancakes 45

Meatball Soup 46

Mu Shu Vegetables 47

No-cook Chocolate Pudding 48

Pear, Grape, and Cucumber Salad 49

Pita Pizza 50

Popcorn and Toppings 51

Salsa Fresca 52

Sautéed Bananas 53

Sesame Chicken Stir-Fry 54

Spaghetti with Meat Sauce 55

Spiced Trail Mix 56

Spinach and Citrus Salad 57

Spring Spread 58

Three Bean Chili 59

Turkey Apple Sausage Muffin Sandwiches 60

Un-Fried Rice 61

Vegetable Noodle Bowl 62

Vegetarian Sushi Roll 63

Veggie Scramble 64

Whole Wheat Pancake 65

Yogurt Parfait 66

Write Your Own Recipe: Oven-baked Omelette (a.k.a. Frittata) 67

Write your Own Recipe: Cheesy Baked Pasta 68

Write Your Own Recipe: Dinner Salad 69

Write your Own Recipe: Fried "Rice" 70

Recipe Template 71

EatFresh.org 72

Mindfulness Activities 73

Soup Bowl Breathing 74

5-4-3-2-1 75

Self Holding 76

Mindful Eating 77

WORKSHOP ACTIVITIES

CONVERSATION QUESTIONS: EXPLORING OUR FOOD HISTORIES

1. What is one food you associate with your childhood? Why?

2. What is most important to you about food?

3. Think of a time in your childhood when someone was cooking. What do you remember about it?

4. What is your favorite comfort food—something you crave when you are stressed or emotional?

5. Who were the caregivers growing up? How did they show love?

6. How did you learn about food and cooking? Who did you learn from?

7. Who have you taught about food and cooking?

8. Describe a favorite food memory. What made that moment special?

9. Who is your role model for self-care? Why?

10. What health issues run in your family, and how are you trying to break the cycle?

11. How have your nutritional needs and habits changed throughout your life?

12. What is the worst thing you ever ate?

T-REX IN TRAFFIC

Check out how T-Rex thinks and feels in these situations, then use the space on the next page to consider your responses.

TEA time ROOARR!

T-Rex is drinking a cup of her favorite tea. She thinks of a funny joke from her best friend. She feels safe and relaxed.

TRAFFIC TIME — ROARRR

T-Rex is stuck in traffic. "I'm going to be late! I'm going to be late!" She feels stressed.

Draw yourself feeling safe and relaxed.
Add labels to tell what you are thinking and feeling.

Draw yourself under stress.
Add labels to tell what you are thinking and feeling.

STRESS AND YOUR BODY

WORKSHOP ACTIVITIES

💡 *The human body is built to handle stress... some of the time. Common symptoms of short-term stress include:*

The **head** may start to hurt; some people become extra sensitive to light and sound

The **brain** may get distracted with repetitive thoughts, making it difficult to concentrate

Vision may get blurry, eyelids may twitch, or **eyes** may hurt

Teeth may clench and the mouth may dry out

Skin may get pale, sweaty, or flushed

Muscles may tense or tremble

Breathing may speed up and become shallow; some people hold their breath

Heart rate increases along with blood pressure; this makes it difficult to sleep

Appetite may go up or down; some people experience nausea or even stomach pain

Bowel and bladder control are reduced during extreme stress

Positive Stress

This stress response isn't always damaging. **Positive stress** occurs with a change or situation you want, such as starting a new job or traveling to a new place. In these situations, a little stress can be motivating.

Tolerable Stress

Tolerable stress occurs when our bodies respond to more serious threats, such as injury or arguments, but return to a calm state easily. Coping skills, loving support, and good health all help the body return to a calm state.

Toxic Stress

When stress is very severe or lasting, however, the body cannot easily return to a calm state. This is **toxic stress**. Over time, toxic stress can lead to serious health problems.

© 2020 Leah's Pantry | *Around the Table: Nourishing Families*

CONVERSATION QUESTIONS: FEEDING OUR FAMILIES

1. How do you encourage your children to eat?

2. How do you make sure your kids are developing healthy eating habits?

3. What about your family's life and routines that enhances your peace and vitality?

4. What is most challenging about feeding your family a nutritious meal?

5. Who cooks in your household? Do family members help out?

6. What does good nourishment mean to you?

7. Are there certain food you don't eat or don't allow your children to eat?

8. Do you find it easier to care for others, or for yourself?

9. What are you most proud of as a parent or caregiver?

10. Do you ever feel judged by others for how you feed yourself or your family? Do you ever find yourself judging others?

11. Do you cook for others? What do you like about doing it? What don't you like about doing it?

12. What is your family's "go-to" meal (an everyday meal they like to have the most)?

13. How do you recognize signs of stress in your family and what do you do about them?

FOOD, MOOD, AND ENERGY

Did you know? A good balanced diet is like building a fire with logs instead of sticks—your fire will burn bigger and longer.

Many people crave **sugar**, **caffeine**, or **highly processed snacks** when stressed, tired, or "down." These provide quick energy or pleasure. But they can also cause a crash when the energy wears off, ultimately making energy or mood even worse. Or they may skip meals when anxious, tired, or in a hurry. This can also cause mood or energy crashes and lead to overeating unhealthy food later.

☑ *Improve your mood and energy with good food.*

A diet rich in **healthy fats** and **fiber**, such as found in whole grains, nuts, and seeds, helps you stay full for hours so your energy doesn't crash. **Protein** fills you up and provides amino acids needed for steady moods.

Vitamins and **minerals** from colorful fruits and vegetables can help the body stay strong and adapt to stress. For example:

- » **Vitamins A** and **C** are found in many red and orange fruits and vegetables. They protect you from illness as well as fight inflammation (irritation) so your body feels its best.
- » **B vitamins** are known as "stress vitamins" because they are so important in helping your body adapt to changes. These are found in dark leafy greens, as well as nuts, seeds, whole grains, and some animal products.

There are many more vitamins and minerals found in fruits and vegetables. That's why doctors recommend: "**Eat a rainbow of fruits and vegetables every day!**"

If you are feeling low energy, unfocused, moody, or agitated, try getting hydrated. **Water** helps to bring nutrients to your muscles so your body can feel more energized. Also, your brain is mostly water, so drinking water can help:

- » improve concentration, memory, and learning
- » balance your mood and emotions

Eating balanced snacks or meals regularly during your day can keep your energy and mood from plummeting.

☑ *Now read about some people struggling with mood and energy, on the following page.*

WORKSHOP ACTIVITIES

What advice would you give to the people below?

Alicia tries to be health conscious but she is very busy and stressed as the single mother to twin 10-year-old boys. She eats a piece of fruit before work and sometimes buys a soup or salad for lunch. In the afternoon, she buys a large iced mocha for an energy boost to finish the work day, pick up her kids at school and prepare dinner. However, she's so hungry by evening that in addition to her own dinner, she tends to eat her kids' leftovers and then snack on chips or cookies while doing the dishes. Sometimes she also has a hard time falling asleep, even after her busy day.

What are some healthy ways Alicia can improve her energy to get through the day?

- ☐ Eat bigger, balanced meals earlier in the day.
- ☐ Keep healthy snacks around, like nuts or cut vegetables, so she can eat these at night instead of chips.
- ☐ Skip afternoon caffeinated drinks and nighttime sugary treats for a better night's sleep.
- ☐ Something else: _____

Mark is proud of his ability to work long hours and support his family, including his kids and elderly mother who lives with them. But every day when his alarm goes off at 6am, he's cranky. He doesn't like to eat breakfast early, so grabs a large coffee and he waits until his lunch break from work at 1pm to eat. Then he goes out to get his favorite food-- cheeseburgers, fries, and a diet coke. Afterwards he feels much better for a little while. But by late afternoon he's cranky again. He drinks sodas throughout the day whenever he's thirsty. By the time he gets home from work around 10pm, he's extremely hungry but doesn't have energy to put together a meal; instead he eats a big bowl of cereal before falling asleep in front of the TV.

What could Mark do to have more steady moods throughout the day?

- ☐ Eat a light but nourishing breakfast such as yogurt or whole grain cereal.
- ☐ Drink more water throughout the day instead of caffeinated drinks.
- ☐ Keep some healthy microwave meals or canned soup on hand to eat at night instead of cereal.
- ☐ Something else: _____

✓ *Now write a case study about yourself in the style of the ones above.*

What are your energy and mood challenges? What part do your eating and drinking habits play? If you can, think of one or two simple ways you could help improve your mood and energy.

TOXIC STRESS: AWARENESS AND RESILIENCE

Some stress is normal and not necessarily damaging. But stress begins to harm our health when it is recurring or drawn out over a long time.

Toxic stress is the body's response to severe or lasting stress. This may also be known as chronic stress. Taking care of ourselves and our families with gentleness and compassion can help reduce the effects of toxic stress and build resilience. There are many causes of toxic stress.

For example, toxic stress can occur when:

- feeling unsafe at home, at work, or at school
- experiencing violence or threats of violence
- having trouble paying your bills or finding enough food to eat regularly
- a close family member is incarcerated
- worrying about having a place to live
- you or a family member have poor health or is disabled
- you don't have a reliable caregiver or support system

Living with Toxic Stress

It may be hard to recognize that these symptoms in children and adults are the result of toxic stress. Growing up or living with toxic stress can cause stress responses such as:

- easily feeling overwhelmed and feeling not able to cope
- aggression or "shutting down"/withdrawal
- "numbing out" with substances or activities (including with media and screens)
- hormone disruption that can lead to early puberty, excessive weight gain, and other health issues
- high blood pressure, diabetes, or heart disease
- trouble staying focused or learning
- mood swings
- sleep issues
- overeating or eating disorders
- compulsive behaviors or addictions
- fear and anxiety
- frequent or chronic illnesses
- chronic colds, headaches, or pain

☑ **How can these stress responses prevent someone from doing things they want or need to do?**

Caregiving and Toxic Stress

Caregiving is an ongoing, demanding job. Those who have experienced toxic stress may find it even harder to stay calm and cope. Their minds and bodies may respond to small problems as if they were big ones. They may get anxious, threatened, and hyper-vigilant even when in a safe and calm place. If someone is caring for children who are stressed too, they may feel even more overwhelmed by the children's symptoms and behaviors. Chronic/toxic stress in an adult may also lead to:

- a limited ability to respond to the needs of your children or family
- difficulty modeling good skills and behavior for children
- difficulty looking after your own health and wellbeing
- memory and concentration problems
- irregular eating habits or overeating (especially fatty or sugary foods)

> **Sleep, exercise, good nourishment, loving relationships, and connecting with others can all help reduce the effects on your and your loved ones' health.**

Brainstorm: Responding to Toxic Stress

1 What are some ways that toxic stress can affect how a person nourishes themselves?

2 Could understanding your stress response help you take better take care of your or your family's health and wellbeing? How?

3 What are some positive ways we can use food or meal time to help ourselves or our families deal with toxic stress? What about some non-food ways?

☑ *There are ways to get support so you can reduce the impact of toxic stress on your health and family:*

- If you or your children have or are dealing with the effects of toxic stress, it is important that you get help and support. Talk to your doctor or a counselor.
- Many areas have 211 or 311 services that can connect you with services such as food assistance, housing assistance, and legal help.
- Check out stresshealth.org and acesconnection.com for more information about toxic stress and adversity.

CONVERSATION QUESTIONS: CREATING A LOVING FOOD ENVIRONMENT

1. What are your meal time rituals?

2. What kind of eating environment does your family enjoy the most?

3. What foods say "love" to you?

4. Are there picky eaters in your home? What helps and what doesn't?

5. What does your family like to talk about when you are eating or spending time together?

6. What happens when a family member doesn't like something that's being served for dinner?

7. How do you know when food is made or offered with love?

8. Do family members share meal preparation or clean up responsibilities?

9. What opportunities does your family have to eat a meal together? What can get in the way of eating together?

10. What makes a dinner table appealing?

11. How does your family begin a meal? How do they know when meal time is over?

12. Describe a dish you like that someone else in your family makes.

13. What do you do when everyone in your household likes or eats different things?

14. How does your family celebrate with food? How about without food?

FOOD PREP: IT'S A FAMILY AFFAIR

Kids are more likely to try foods they've helped choose and prepare. (Adults too!) Review these tips for involving the whole family in meal planning and preparation. Check off any you could do with those in your home.

PRESCHOOLERS

- ☐ spread nut butter or cream cheese on bread
- ☐ help wash veggies and fruit
- ☐ help select foods at the grocery store
- ☐ carry unbreakable items to and from the table
- ☐ serve themselves at the table (with help)
- ☐ pour liquids into batters (you measure)
- ☐ stir or mix batter, or other wet or dry ingredients
- ☐ knead bread dough; press cookie cutters into dough or bread
- ☐ use a damp sponge to wipe counters, tables and chairs after eating

❋ *Remember: You decide what and when kids eat, they decide how much. Children are more likely to develop good eating habits when they are able to manage their own appetites. New foods take time; patience and repeated exposure works better than pressure!*

ELEMENTARY SCHOOL KIDS

- ☐ tell other family members what's in a recipe, or why foods are healthy
- ☐ practice cutting softer ingredients with a butter knife, a strong plastic knife, or even a paring knife (supervise when using sharp knives)
- ☐ grate or mash soft fruits, veggies and beans; juice lemons or limes; crack eggs
- ☐ serve themselves and others at the table
- ☐ begin to read recipes and measure with cups and spoons
- ☐ begin to learn stovetop and oven basics (with supervision)
- ☐ set or clear the table; help with washing, drying, and putting away dishes

❋ *Remember: Let your kids be "produce pickers" by choosing fruits and veggies at the store. Try reintroducing foods they might not have liked when they were younger. As they get older, they are more able to eat stronger flavored foods.*

OLDER KIDS, TEENS, AND ADULTS

- ☐ find and choose recipes; prepare a whole meal; help meal plan
- ☐ help with grocery shopping, including making a list and budget
- ☐ chop ingredients with a knife (supervise as needed)
- ☐ use kitchen appliances
- ☐ read food labels for ingredients, nutrients, and health claims
- ☐ set/clear the table; wash, dry, and put away dishes

❋ *Remember: Youth are naturally curious about cooking and like to be creative. This may seem like a hassle at times, but it means they're paying attention to food—which is healthy in the long run!*

ANYONE

- ☐ say "grace" or offer thanks for a meal
- ☐ decorate or make the table look special
- ☐ put away tech devices at mealtime
- ☐ wait for others to be seated and served before eating

✔ *What ideas would you add?*

CONVERSATION QUESTIONS: NOURISHMENT AWAY FROM HOME

1. What is the most challenging or stressful thing about going to the grocery store?

2. What is your family's favorite eating out experience or event?

3. How are your food decisions different when eating out vs. home?

4. Do you care about name brands when you grocery shop?

5. How does money influence your food choices away from home?

6. When you feel stress at the grocery store or in a restaurant, what can help?

7. How does the label or packaging on a food product influence your decision to purchase it?

8. What is the most important thing you do to keep within your food budget?

9. How do you think advertisements affect your buying or eating habits?

10. What can make eating out a stressful experience?

11. Which one of these is most important to you: customer service, food quality, or affordability?

12. What do you and your family look forward to the most when you eat out?

13. Do you or anyone in your family make a shopping list or plan your meals ahead of time? Do you see any advantages or disadvantages?

14. Do you feel confident or successful when you grocery shop? What are your best strategies?

OUTSMART THE GROCERY STORE

How does the layout of your grocery store shape your choices?
Where are the healthiest foods are located?
Are products displayed at the ends of aisles always on sale?
Why are candy and magazines always near the register?
What types of food do you think make the store a higher profit?

TIPS

- **Make a plan, come with a list.** Planning your meals ahead of time and using a shopping list saves time, saves money, and encourages healthier eating.

- **Compare unit prices.** Unit prices allow you to compare the price of two packages that may contain a different amount of food. Larger packages often have lower unit prices; however, be sure to consider whether you'll be able to eat the entire amount before it goes bad.

32 OZ LF YOGURT	6 OZ LF YOGURT
UNIT PRICE $0.05 per oz — RETAIL PRICE $1.62	UNIT PRICE $0.12 per oz — RETAIL PRICE $0.72

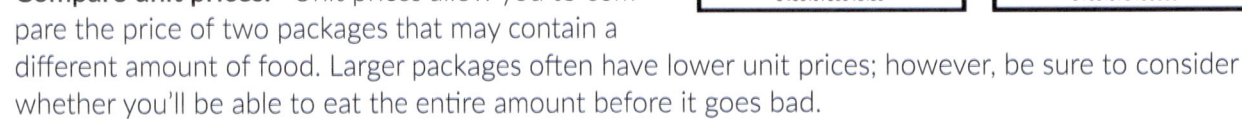

- **Look up and look down.** The most expensive or profitable products are often placed right at eye level. Look on the higher and lower shelves to see if there are cheaper alternatives. Also, watch out for special displays at the end of the aisle. That doesn't mean it's on sale. Sometimes it's just there to get you to buy it.

- **Compare brands.** Store brands and generic products are often identical to name brand products in everything but price. Look at the ingredients list to compare.

- **Coupons and sales can be worth it... sometimes.** Coupons and specials can be a good way to save money—when you use them wisely. Stick to buying bargain items that are already on your list.

- **Don't pay for empty calories and low quality ingredients.** Processed foods often contain ingredients that don't cost the manufacturer a lot of money but they can make a big profit from it. A lot of junk food masquerades as healthy with meaningless front-of-packaging labels like "natural." Remember to check the labels.

DON'T LABEL ME!

👍 *How do you think the design or wording on the front of the package tries to influence you to buy it? Do you look at labels on food packages when you are shopping? What do you usually look for? What one item is most useful for you to look at?*

☑ *Use this glossary to explore terms typically found on a food label.*

1. **calories**—the energy provided by a food. *Eating more calories than your body uses leads to weight gain.*

2. **carbohydrate**—a nutrient with calories. This is the body's main source of energy. *Carbohydrate-containing foods with fiber provide longer lasting energy.*

3. **fat**—a nutrient that gives a concentrated form of energy, helps absorb other nutrients, and helps build/repair many parts of the body. *High fat foods are also high in calories. Foods labeled low-fat, reduced-fat, or fat-free may have added sugars or other ingredients to make up for the loss of texture or flavor.*

4. **fiber**—a form of carbohydrate that carries water and waste through the body. *Fiber helps you feel full longer, helps lower cholesterol, and controls blood sugar levels.*

5. **gluten-free**—foods without gluten, a type of protein found in some grains (especially wheat). *Some people cannot digest gluten properly or are allergic.*

6. **GMO-free**—a food without ingredients that had its genetic material artificially manipulated to produce genetically modified organisms. *Some people choose non-GMO foods out of concern for possible unknown effects on the earth and human health.*

7. **organic**—foods grown and processed without the use of chemicals. *People may choose organic foods to avoid chemicals for themselves, or to protect farm workers and the earth from chemicals.*

8. **protein**—a nutrient that forms the building blocks of cells, muscles, and tissues. *In addition to animal foods, many plant foods also contain protein.*

9. **sodium, a.k.a. "salt"**—a mineral the body needs in small amounts. *Too much is unhealthy for people with high blood pressure. Processed foods often have a lot.*

10. **sugars**—a form of carbohydrate that gives instant energy. *Processed foods may have unhealthy amounts of added sugars.*

11. **vegan**—foods without any animal products (including eggs or dairy) and made without harming animals.

12. **vitamins and minerals**—compounds the brain and body need in small amounts to function well. *Whole foods and minimally-processed foods contain more vitamins and minerals.*

13. **whole grains**—grains that have not had anything removed in processing. *These have more vitamins, minerals, and fiber than "refined" white grains like white flour and white rice.*

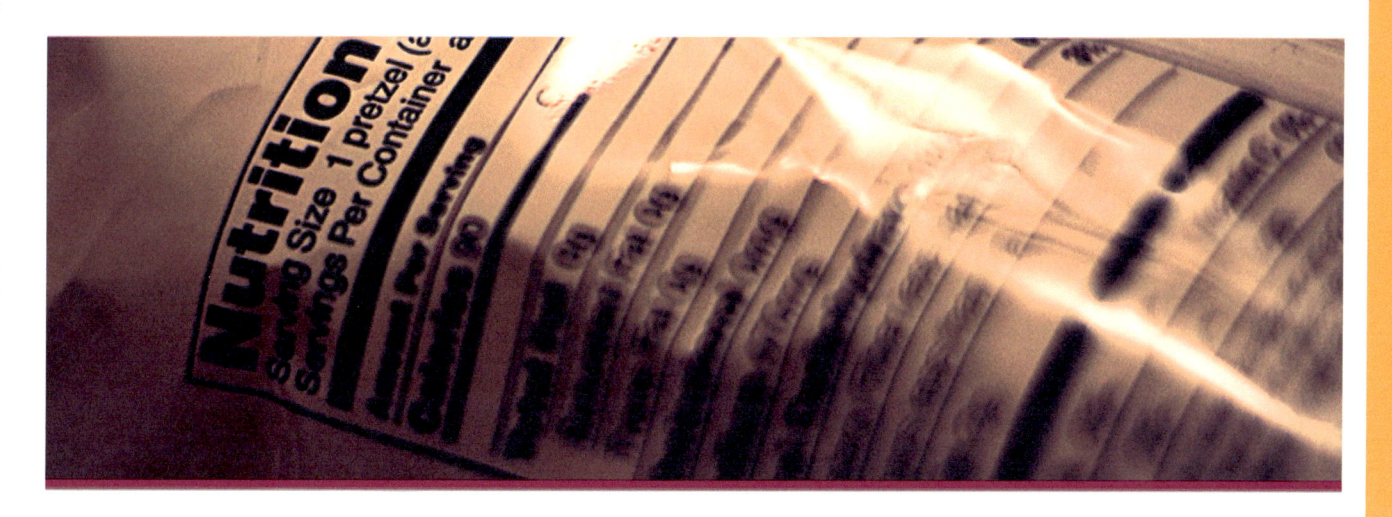

CANNED, BOXED, AND BAGGED

Do you know how to make healthy choices regarding packaged foods?

❶ Can you tell what plant or animal it came from?

Choose foods made from ingredients you can picture in their raw state or growing in nature. If you see something you can't pronounce and think it was made in a lab, beware.

❷ Don't be fooled by big health claims or slogans on a package.

They can distract you from something less healthy, such as high sodium or sugar content.

❸ Avoid foods with sugar listed in the first three ingredients.

Also, look for "added sugars" on the nutrition facts label. Be aware that sugar can have a variety of names. Look at the list for some examples. ➤

❹ Look for 100% whole grain foods.

Look for the whole grain label or the word "whole" in the first ingredient. Examples include: whole wheat, whole oats, whole grain corn, and brown rice.

WORDS FOR SUGAR

- » Honey
- » Brown sugar
- » Dextrose
- » Sucrose
- » High fructose corn syrup
- » Fruit juice concentrate
- » Barley malt
- » Cane juice
- » Molasses
- » Brown rice syrup
- » Glucose
- » Caramel

CONVERSATION QUESTIONS: NOURISHMENT IN OUR COMMUNITIES

1. Describe your community. What gives you a sense of belonging to your community?

2. Where do you get affordable healthy food in your community? Is it hard or easy to find?

3. Who in your community may be struggling to get good food? What resources are available to them?

4. Does your neighborhood provide the types of food stores and restaurants you want? What types of stores or restaurants would you want for your community?

5. Where do you look for information about health and nutrition?

6. What do you think about the nutrition and health information and resources that are available in your community? Are they helpful?

7. Does food play a part in building and connecting your community? How?

8. Where and what kinds of food advertisements do you see in your neighborhood? What messages do they convey to you and your neighbors?

9. Do you trust your doctor enough to share your nutrition concerns such as weight, diet, health conditions, or getting enough food?

10. What are some "red flags" to identify nutrition information or advice that isn't good?

11. How do the people in your life or community talk about weight, diet, nutrition or food? Do you feel positively or negatively about these conversations?

12. What do you think is the biggest food or nutrition problem facing your community?

13. What would you do to help your community become healthier or improve it's vitality?

14. What could community leaders, organizations, businesses, or institutions do to help your community be healthier and improve its vitality?

24 MY FAMILY COAT OF ARMS

WORKSHOP ACTIVITIES

💡 *What symbolizes the values and beliefs that are meaningful to you and your family?*

☑ In medieval Europe, coats of arms were worn into battle by noble families. Design a coat of arms for you and your family, to represent the values, beliefs, skills, strengths, and practices that are important to you, to keep you and your family nourished, healthy, and resilient.

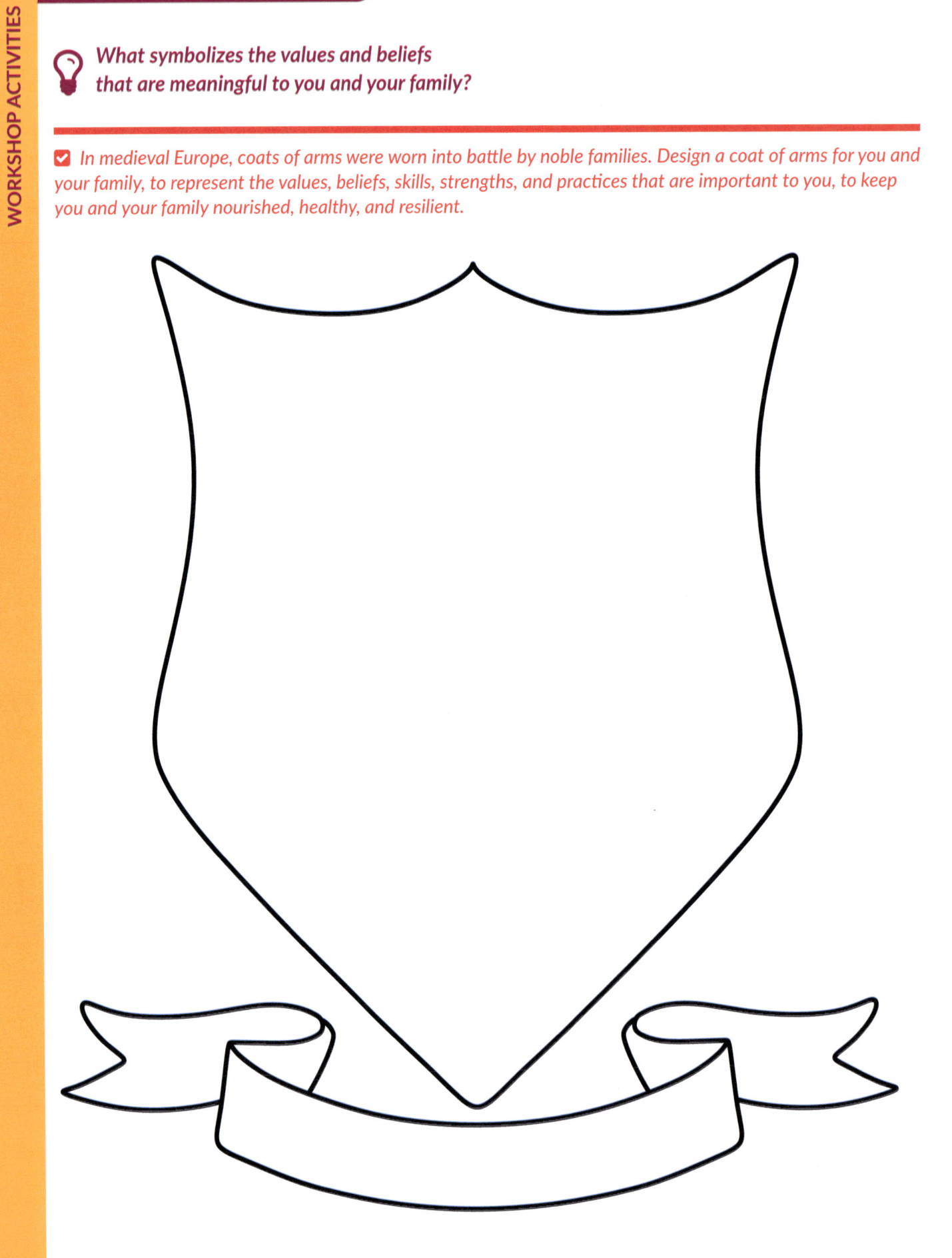

© 2020 Leah's Pantry | Around the Table: Nourishing Families

RECIPES AND MENU PLANNING

INDEX OF FAMILY FRIENDLY RECIPES

■ The Rainbow of Fruits and Vegetables

Black Bean and Vegetable Tostada	34
Corn and Black Bean Salad	38
Chicken Caesar Pasta Salad	35
Chicken Lettuce Wraps	36
Fresh Veggies and Dip	41
Korean-Style Vegetable Pancakes	45
Mu Shu Vegetables	47
Pear, Grape, and Cucumber Salad	49
Salsa Fresca	52
Sesame Chicken Stir-Fry	54
Spinach and Citrus Salad	57
Spring Spread	58
Un-Fried Rice	61
Vegetable Noodle Bowl	62
Vegetarian Sushi Roll	63
Write Your Own Recipe: Dinner Salad	69

■ Delicious Whole Grains

Banana Sushi	33
Egg Burritos	39
Pita Pizza	50
Un-Fried Rice	61
Vegetarian Sushi Roll	63
Whole Wheat Pancake	65
Yogurt Parfait	66

■ Healthy Breakfasts

Banana Sushi	33
Egg Burritos	39
Green Smoothie	44
Turkey Apple Sausage Muffin Sandwiches	60
Veggie Scramble	64
Whole Wheat Pancake	65
Yogurt Parfait	66

■ Rethink Your Drink, Treats, and Snacks (Reducing Added Sugars, Salt, and Fat)

Baby Tomato Bites	32
Banana Sushi	33
Fresh Veggies and Dip	41
Fruit Crisp	42
Fudgy Fruit	43
No-cook Chocolate Pudding	48
Popcorn and Toppings	51
Salsa Fresca	52
Sautéed Bananas	53
Spiced Trail Mix	56
Spring Spread	58
Vegetarian Sushi Roll	63
Yogurt Parfait	66

■ Healthy One-Dish Meals

Chicken Caesar Pasta Salad	35
Corn and Black Bean Salad	38
Meatball Soup	46
Mu Shu Vegetables	47
Spaghetti with Meat Sauce	55
Three Bean Chili	59
Un-Fried Rice	61
Veggie Scramble	64
Write Your Own Recipe: Oven-baked Omelette (a.k.a. Frittata)	67
Write your Own Recipe: Fried "Rice"	70
Write your Own Recipe: Cheesy Baked Pasta	68

■ Kids in the Kitchen: Simple Recipes for Young Cooks

Baby Tomato Bites	32
Banana Sushi	33
Egg Burritos	39
Fresh Veggies and Dip	41
Fudgy Fruit	43
Green Smoothie	44
No-cook Chocolate Pudding	48
Pear, Grape, and Cucumber Salad	49

Pita Pizza 50

Popcorn and Toppings 51

Spiced Trail Mix 56

Spinach and Citrus Salad 57

Spring Spread 58

Vegetarian Sushi Roll 63

Veggie Scramble 64

Whole Wheat Pancake 65

Yogurt Parfait 66

■ Whole Foods Instead of Fast Foods

Black Bean and Vegetable Tostada 34

Chicken Lettuce Wraps 36

Chicken Soft Tacos 37

Egg Burritos 39

Fish Tacos 40

Korean-Style Vegetable Pancakes 45

Pita Pizza 50

Turkey Apple Sausage Muffin Sandwiches 60

Un-Fried Rice 61

■ Write Your Own Recipe

Write Your Own Recipe: Oven-baked Omelette (a.k.a. Frittata) 67

Write your Own Recipe: Cheesy Baked Pasta 68

Write Your Own Recipe: Dinner Salad 69

Write your Own Recipe: Fried "Rice" 70

Recipe Template 71

MEAL PLANNER & BUDGET TRACKER

MEAL PLAN	SHOPPING LIST					BUDGETING	
Recipe/Dish	Produce	Meat	Dairy	Dry, Canned, Boxed	Other	Total Bill	Cost Per Person

RECIPES AND MENU PLANNING

MEAL PLAN	SHOPPING LIST					BUDGETING	
Recipe/Dish	Produce	Meat	Dairy	Dry, Canned, Boxed	Other	Total Bill	Cost Per Person

MEAL PLAN	SHOPPING LIST					BUDGETING	
Recipe/Dish	Produce	Meat	Dairy	Dry, Canned, Boxed	Other	Total Bill	Cost Per Person

RECIPES AND MENU PLANNING

BABY TOMATO BITES

Ready In 15 min. **Serves** 6

With ingredients from three of five food groups, this recipe makes a balanced snack or a light meal. You may substitute 2 teaspoons dried oregano if fresh basil is not available.

Ingredients

- 12 (4-inch) slices of French bread
- ¼ c. shredded low-fat mozzarella cheese
- 5 small tomatoes, *diced very small*
- ½ tsp. black pepper
- ¼ tsp. salt
- 8 basil leaves, *chopped*

Directions

1. Preheat oven to 300°F.
2. Place thin layer of mozzarella cheese on each slice of bread.
3. Toast French bread slices in oven until cheese melts, about 5-8 minutes.
4. Mix diced tomatoes, pepper, salt, and basil.
5. Place diced tomatoes on top of toasts. Serve immediately.

Nutrition Info *per 2-slice serving*

Total calories: 190
Carbohydrates: 33 g
Total fat: 3 g
Saturated fat: 1 g
Protein: 9 g
Fiber: 2 g
Sodium: 443 mg

How would you adapt this recipe for your family?

How might family members help you with this recipe?

What could you serve this with to make it a meal?

BANANA SUSHI

Ready In 5 min. | **Serves** 2

This easy dish makes a great meal or snack for any time of day. It is more filling and provides longer-lasting energy than some other common snacks or breakfasts. Whole grain bread and tortillas contain more fiber than ones made from white flour. That's why whole grain foods like the tortillas in this recipe may help you stay full for longer. Read ingredients lists to identify whole grain foods; you should see the word "whole" in the first ingredient, for example, "whole wheat flour" or "whole grain oats."

Ingredients

- 1 8-inch soft whole wheat tortilla
- 2 tbsp. all-natural peanut butter
- Cinnamon to taste
- 1 banana, *peeled*
- 1 tbsp. raisins or chopped nuts (optional)

Directions

1. Spread a layer of peanut butter across the tortilla. Leave a gap at the edge about as wide as your fingertip.
2. Sprinkle with raisins or nuts, if using.
3. Shake cinnamon on top of the peanut butter.
4. Place the peeled banana in the middle of the tortilla.
5. Roll the tortilla tightly.
6. Cut into 8 pieces.

❋ **Tip:** Try to find a peanut butter with nothing in it but peanuts and salt. Avoid peanut butter with added oil or sugar.

Nutrition Info *per 4-piece serving*

Total calories: 232
Carbohydrates: 31 g
Total fat: 11 g
Saturated fat: 3 g
Protein: 7 g
Fiber: 5 g
Sodium: 185 mg

How would you adapt this recipe for your family?

How might family members help you with this recipe?

What are some other whole grain foods that your family eats or would be willing to try?

BLACK BEAN AND VEGETABLE TOSTADA

Ready In 25 min. **Serves** 5

These colorful tostadas are almost like fast food tacos, except you know exactly what's in them! Red bell peppers and tomatoes are a good source of vitamin C for your immune system; tomatoes and cilantro provide vitamin K for your blood; and beans provide plenty of fiber to keep you full.

Ingredients

- 1 tbsp. oil, *separated*
- ¼ c. chopped onion
- 1 small red bell pepper, *diced*
- 1 c. canned, defrosted, or fresh corn kernels
- 1 medium zucchini or yellow squash, *diced*
- 3 cloves garlic, *finely minced*
- 1½ c. vegetarian refried black or pinto beans
- 5 crispy corn tostada shells
- 4 medium tomatoes, *chopped*
- 1 small red onion, *chopped*
- 1 bunch of cilantro, *chopped*
- ½ cup crumbled Mexican cheese or mild feta

Directions

1. Heat 2 tsp. oil in medium skillet. Add onion, bell peppers, corn, and zucchini/yellow squash. Cook, stirring occasionally, until vegetables are softened, about 6 minutes. Set aside.
2. Heat 1 tsp. oil in medium skillet. Add chopped garlic. Cook for 30 seconds. Add can of refried beans. Mix beans and garlic together until smooth and heated through. Set aside.
3. Spread a thin layer of the bean and garlic mixture on top of a tostada. Add a spoonful of the cooked vegetables. Top the with tomatoes, red onion, cilantro, and cheese.
4. Eat by picking up the tostada with both hands.

✻ *Tip: Make your own tostada shell: Spread out 5 corn tortillas on a foil lined baking sheet. Brush lightly with oil and sprinkle with salt (optional). Bake the tortillas in a preheated 400 degree oven for approximately four minutes per side, or until they are crispy and golden on each side.*

Nutrition Info *per tostada*

Total calories: 233
Carbohydrates: 37 g
Total fat: 8 g
Saturated fat: 2 g
Protein: 8 g
Fiber: 7 g
Sodium: 467 mg
Added Sugar: <1g

💡 Do you have any friends or family members who might be encouraged to eat vegetables by this recipe?

What other favorite foods could you add fresh vegetables or beans to?

How might you change this recipe if you were in a hurry?

CHICKEN CAESAR PASTA SALAD

Ready In 25 min. **Serves** 6

This meal salad is a hit even with people who say they don't like green salad. You can feel good about serving it because it contains all five food groups, whole grains, and colorful vegetables. It's also a great way to use leftover chicken. If you have picky eaters, keep the ingredients separate and let everyone build their own.

Ingredients

- 3 c. grilled chicken breast or roasted chicken breast, *chopped or shredded*
- 2 c. dry whole grain penne pasta
- 6 c. Romaine lettuce, *chopped*
- 1½ c. cherry tomatoes halves
- ½ c. fresh basil, *chopped*
- ½ c. green onions, *chopped*
- ¼ c. fresh parsley, *chopped*
- 3 oz. Feta cheese, *crumbled*
- 2 garlic cloves, *minced*
- ⅓ c. Caesar dressing

Directions

1. Cook pasta by following package directions, drain and lightly rinse with cold water.
2. In a large bowl: combine all ingredients and toss until all ingredients are coated with dressing.
3. Serve immediately.

✸ **Tips:** *Experiment with the salad…*
Substitute the basil/parsley with cilantro
Substitute the feta cheese for one of your choice
Try a different type of pasta
Try it with your favorite dressing
Try it with sliced olives

Nutrition Info *per ⅙ serving*

Total calories: 346
Carbohydrates: 26 g
Total fat: 14 g
Saturated fat: 4 g
Protein: 29 g
Fiber: 5 g
Sodium: 348 mg

How would you adapt this recipe for your family?

How might family members help you with this recipe?

Do you think family members would notice that this recipe is made with whole grain noodles? Why or why not?

CHICKEN LETTUCE WRAPS

Ready In 20 min. **Serves** 6

Eating a Rainbow of Fruits and Vegetables is one way to get a variety of vitamins every day. In this simple recipe, ground chicken is mixed with colorful vegetables, cooked and wrapped in crunchy green lettuce. Family members will enjoy filling their own lettuce wraps.

Ingredients

- 1 pound ground chicken
- ½ onion, *chopped*
- Salt and black pepper, *to taste*
- 2 garlic cloves minced, or 1 tsp. garlic powder
- 1 inch piece of ginger, *peeled and minced*, or ½ tsp. ginger powder
- 1 c. celery, *chopped*
- 1 carrot, *grated*
- ¼ c. sesame salad dressing or teriyaki sauce
- 12 large outer lettuce leaves, *rinsed and patted dry*
- 1 tsp. red chili powder or chili flakes (optional)
- ¼ c. chopped peanuts (optional)

Stove Top or Skillet Directions

1. Heat 1 tbsp. oil in the bottom of a skillet.
2. Add onion and cook for 3 minutes.
3. Add garlic, ginger, celery, and ground chicken.
4. Sauté until chicken is cooked through.
5. Add carrot, dressing or sauce, and optional chili flakes. Cook for 2 more minutes.
6. Roll about ½ c. of filling into each lettuce leaf like a taco. Sprinkle with optional peanuts.

Microwave Directions

1. Microwave chicken and onion for 2 minutes.
2. Stir in garlic, ginger, and celery. Microwave 2-3 more minutes until cooked.
3. Add carrots, dressing or sauce, and optional chili flakes. Cook for 2 more minutes.
4. Roll about ½ c. filling in each lettuce leaf like a taco. Sprinkle with optional crushed peanuts.

Tip: You can make your own teriyaki sauce. Heat 2 tbsp. soy sauce with 1 tbsp. sugar and 1 tbsp. white vinegar in your microwave for about 1 minute. Stir to dissolve the sugar.

Nutrition Info *per 2-wrap serving*

Total calories: 157 **Total fat:** 10 g **Protein:** 12 g **Sodium:** 183 mg
Carbohydrates: 6 g **Saturated fat:** 2 g **Fiber:** 2 g

How do you know when ground meats are cooked through?

What vegetables could you add to make this dish even more colorful?

CHICKEN SOFT TACOS

Ready In 20 min.
Serves 8

These tacos are a nutritious, filling choice for anyone looking to cut down on red meat or salty fast foods. They include healthy, brain boosting fat from avocados as well as fiber, vitamins and minerals from colorful vegetables.

Ingredients

- 3 tbsp. balsamic vinegar
- 2 tbsp. canned chipotle peppers in adobo sauce, *finely chopped*
- 3 tsp. garlic salt
- 4 c. cooked skinless chicken, *chopped or shredded*
- 4 c. shredded cabbage or prepared coleslaw mix
- 1 c. red onion, *finely diced*
- 16 (6-inch) corn tortillas
- 1 c. Mexican-style or Feta cheese, *crumbled*
- 2 avocados, *peeled, pitted, chopped*

Directions

1. In a medium bowl, mix together balsamic vinegar, chipotle peppers, and garlic salt. Add in chicken, cabbage, and onion, mix well.
2. To warm tortillas, heat in a hot skillet for 1 minute on each side. Or place tortillas on a large plate and top with a damp paper towel. Microwave on high for 2 minutes or until tortillas are warm.
3. Spoon filling into warm tortillas and top with cheese and avocado. Serve immediately.

❋ **Tip:** You can substitute jarred salsa if you can't find canned chipotle peppers in adobo.

Nutrition Info *per 2-taco serving*

Total calories: 340
Carbohydrates: 32 g
Total fat: 12 g
Saturated fat: 4 g
Protein: 27 g
Fiber: 7 g
Sodium: 360 mg

How would you adapt this recipe for your family?

Why do you think fast food often contains more fat, salt, and sugar than homemade?

What are some advantages and disadvantages of fast food vs. homemade?

CORN AND BLACK BEAN SALAD

Ready In 10 min. | **Serves** 4

Canned beans make a terrific addition to salads. They're an inexpensive way to add protein to a meal and require little preparation. This salad features black beans and a mix of colorful vegetables, so it has lots of fiber to keep you full. It can be eaten as a side or as a complete meatless meal. Chop the vegetables very small and it also makes a great salsa.

Ingredients

- 2 tbsp. extra-virgin olive oil
- Red wine vinegar, *to taste*
- Fresh lime juice, *to taste*
- ½ c. canned black beans, *drained and rinsed*
- ½ c. fresh, defrosted, or canned corn kernels
- ½ c. red or green bell peppers, *chopped*
- ½ c. tomato, *chopped*
- ½ c. red onion, *chopped*
- 1 tsp. cumin
- 1 tsp. chili pepper
- ½ tsp. salt
- ½ tsp. pepper

Directions

1. Mix together beans and vegetables in a large bowl.
2. Toss with olive oil, vinegar, and lime juice.

Nutrition Info *per ½ cup serving*

Total calories: 122
Carbohydrates: 13 g
Total fat: 7 g
Saturated fat: 1 g
Protein: 3 g
Fiber: 3.5 g
Sodium: 186 mg

Which flavors stick out when you eat this recipe? Which ingredients "blend in?"

What are some fun additions or changes you can make to this recipe?

How could you turn this into a main dish?

EGG BURRITOS

Ready In 30 min. | **Serves** 4

Instead of buying frozen or fast food burritos, you can make your own with a lot more flavor and nutrients. These egg burritos can be frozen and reheated for breakfast, dinner, or any time you need a balanced meal on the go. Kids love to help assemble them!

Ingredients

- 3 green onions, *sliced*
- 1 red or green bell pepper, *diced small*
- 1 clove garlic, *minced*
- 1 (15.5-oz) can no-salt added black beans, *drained and rinsed*
- 2 tsp. oil, *divided*
- 4 large eggs
- ¼ c. cilantro, *chopped* (optional)
- ¾ tsp. ground cumin, *divided*
- ¼ tsp. ground black pepper
- 4 (8-inch) whole wheat flour tortillas
- ½ c. low-fat cheddar cheese, *grated*

❋ **Notes:** If you double the recipe, do not double cumin. Also, when a recipe says "divided" or "separated," it means you will use that ingredient in more than one place in the dish, rather than all at once.

Directions

1. Heat oil in a medium skillet over medium heat. Add beans, green onions, bell pepper, and garlic. Cook until peppers are soft, about 3 minutes. Add ½ tsp. ground cumin and black pepper. Transfer mixture to a bowl.
2. In a small bowl, crack eggs. Add remaining ¼ tsp. cumin. Beat mixture lightly with a fork.
3. Wipe out skillet with a paper towel. Heat 1 tsp oil on medium-low. Add egg mixture. Cook, stirring occasionally, until eggs are as firm as you like. If using cilantro, add now.
4. Spoon egg mixture into the center of each tortilla, dividing evenly. Add beans and veggies. Sprinkle cheese on top.
5. Fold tortilla over mixture and serve.

❋ **Tips:** Burritos can be frozen for up to one week. Wrap tightly in plastic wrap, cover with aluminum foil, and freeze. To reheat, remove foil and plastic. Microwave 1 ½ - 2 minutes, turning as needed. Or, remove plastic wrap and re-cover in aluminum foil. Heat in a toaster oven or regular oven at 300° F for about 6 minutes.

Nutrition Info *per burrito*

Total calories: 350　　**Total fat:** 9 g　　**Protein:** 20 g　　**Sodium:** 510 mg
Carbohydrates: 45 g　　**Saturated fat:** 1 g　　**Fiber:** 9 g

What recipe steps could family members help you with?

If you didn't have enough money for all the ingredients, what could you leave out?

How might this recipe be more nutritious than a frozen burrito?

FISH TACOS

Ready In 25 min. **Serves** 6

Fish and shellfish, like used in this recipe, are a great source of protein and healthy fats. Most seafood can be found frozen and is often less expensive than fresh but just as healthy. The seasonings and toppings in this dish make it a tasty way to get family members to eat fish. Serve all the toppings separately so everyone can make their tacos just exactly as they like.

Ingredients

- 1 pound white fish fillets, such as cod, *cut into 1-inch pieces*
- 1 tbsp. olive oil
- 2 tbsp. lemon juice
- 1 tbsp. taco seasoning
- 12 (6-inch) corn tortillas, *warmed*
- 2 c. red or green cabbage, *shredded*
- 2 c. tomatoes, *chopped*
- ½ c. plain Greek yogurt or low-fat sour cream
- Hot sauce, *to taste*
- Lime wedges for serving (optional)

Directions

1. Heat a large skillet.
2. In a medium bowl, combine fish, olive oil, lemon juice, and taco seasoning.
3. Add to skillet and cook, stirring constantly, over medium-high heat for 4 to 5 minutes or until fish flakes easily when tested with a fork.
4. Fill tortillas with fish mixture.
5. Top with cabbage, tomato, Greek yogurt, and hot sauce. Serve with lime wedge for squeezing over, if desired.

Tip: You can make your own flavorful taco seasoning by mixing up powdered chili, garlic, onion, cumin, paprika, dried oregano, and salt.

Nutrition Info *per 2-taco serving*

Total calories: 239
Carbohydrates: 32 g
Total fat: 5 g
Saturated fat: 1 g
Protein: 19 g
Fiber: 4 g
Sodium: 247 mg

How would you adapt this recipe for your family?

How do you know when fish is fully cooked?

What could you serve alongside these tacos?

FRESH VEGGIES AND DIP

Ready In 10 min.
Serves 4

Are there any snacks that fill you up without weighing you down? Raw fruits and vegetables are an ideal way to refuel between meals; they're nutritious and filling without ruining your appetite. However, you may find them boring on their own. If so, try dressing up raw vegetables with a simple dip, such as the one in this recipe.

Ingredients

- ½ c. plain Greek yogurt or low-fat sour cream
- ⅓ c. prepared salsa
- 3 tbsp. green onions, *chopped*
- ½ tsp. garlic salt
- 1 red bell pepper, *cut into strips*
- 2 celery stalks, *cut into sticks*
- 1 c. baby carrots

Directions

1. Put sour cream, salsa, green onions, and garlic salt in a small bowl. Stir well.
2. Serve red bell pepper strips, celery sticks, and baby carrots with dip.

Nutrition Info *per 1 cup serving*

Total calories: 66
Carbohydrates: 12 g
Total fat: <1 g
Saturated fat: <1 g
Protein: 2 g
Fiber: 4.2 g
Sodium: 240 mg

What are some other ways to add flavor to raw fruits and vegetables?

Think of your favorite raw vegetable. How could you prepare/store it for easy snacking?

FRUIT CRISP

Ready In 10 min.+ | **Serves** 4

Oats, spices, fruit baked with a touch of sugar are an easy dessert to make for your friends or family. The best part is that the fiber from the oats, fruit, and nuts (if using) slow down the absorption of the sugar, so you don't get a sugar rush or crash like other desserts. Top this with a little yogurt to make it special.

Ingredients

- 4 c. fruit, *diced or sliced*
- 4 tbsp. soft butter or oil
- 4 tbsp. brown sugar
- 8 tbsp. rolled oats
- 4 tbsp. whole wheat flour
- 1 tsp. ground cinnamon
- 6 tbsp. walnuts, pecans, or almonds, *chopped* (optional)

Microwave Directions

1. Place fruit in a microwave-safe dish.
2. Use a dish that is wide enough so that the fruit is about 1 inch deep in the bottom. Combine remaining ingredients to make oat topping and sprinkle it over the fruit.
3. Microwave on high 1-5 minutes or until fruit is as tender as you like it.

Oven Directions

1. Place fruit in the bottom of a baking dish.
2. In a separate bowl, mix together butter/oil, oats, brown sugar, flour, cinnamon, and nuts.
3. Sprinkle the mixture over the fruit.
4. Bake at 375° F for 45 minutes or until the top is golden brown.

* **Tip:** Frozen fruit works well in this recipe. Just be sure to thaw it before using. Or you can use canned fruit that has been rinsed to remove the sugar.

Nutrition Info *per 1 cup serving*

Total calories: 336
Carbohydrates: 48 g
Total fat: 15 g
Saturated fat: 1 g
Protein: 5 g
Fiber: 6 g
Sodium: 6 mg

What type of fruit do you think would work best in this recipe?

How might family members help you with this recipe?

What special desserts does your family enjoy?

FUDGY FRUIT

Ready In: 15 min. **Serves:** 4

Fresh fruit, when eaten in season, is often sweet enough to make a satisfying dessert. If you like to dress it up however, this recipe for fresh fruit with a chocolate drizzle still has far less added sugar than processed candies, pastries, or ice cream.

Ingredients

- 2 tbsp. semi-sweet chocolate chips
- 2 large bananas, *peeled and cut into quarters*
- 8 large strawberries
- ¼ c. unsalted toasted coconut or chopped nuts (optional)

Directions

1. Place chocolate chips in a small microwave safe bowl. Heat on high for 10 seconds and stir. Repeat until chocolate is melted, about 30 seconds.
2. Place fruit on a small tray covered with a piece of waxed paper. Use a spoon to drizzle the melted chocolate on top of the fruit.
3. Sprinkle the fruit with chopped coconut or nuts.
4. Cover the fruit and place in the refrigerator for 10 minutes or until the chocolate hardens. Serve chilled.

Nutrition Info *per 4-piece serving*

Total calories: 112
Carbohydrates: 25 g
Total fat: 2 g
Saturated fat: 1 g
Protein: 1.6 g
Fiber: 4.7 g
Sodium: 238 mg

What other fruit would you use in this recipe?

How might family members help you with this recipe?

What are foods with natural sugars? How can you identify foods with added sugars?

GREEN SMOOTHIE

Ready In 5 min.
Serves 2

In recent years, bottled juices and smoothies have become more popular. These can be expensive though, and often contain just as much sugar as soft drinks! This smoothie is an inexpensive, nutrient-packed alternative you can make yourself. It's also a great way to add greens to your diet, even if you don't love their flavor. Use at least one kind of frozen fruit to make this cold, thick and creamy.

Ingredients

- 2 large handful raw greens such as spinach or kale (about 1 c.)
- 1 medium banana
- 2 c. other fresh or frozen fruit, *chopped*
- 2 c. milk or milk substitute

Directions

1. Place all ingredients in a blender in the order listed.
2. Blend until smooth and creamy. Add a little water if desired for a thinner smoothie.
3. Serve immediately.

❋ **Tip:** Yellow, green, or orange fruits make this smoothie a pretty color while reds and purples might make it look a little darker or grayer. Regardless, any color fruit tastes delicious!

Nutrition Info *per 2 cup serving*

Total calories: 218
Carbohydrates: 45 g
Total fat: 1.5 g
Saturated fat: <1 g
Protein: 10 g
Fiber: 6 g
Sodium: 129 mg

What could you add to make this even more nutritious?

Do you try sneaking vegetables into your family's diet? What might be the pros and cons of sneaking it in?

KOREAN-STYLE VEGETABLE PANCAKES

Ready In: 35 min. **Serves:** 4

Fresh vegetables, as well as many other plant foods, have protein; in fact, calorie for calorie, some have as much protein as meat! Vegetables also contain fiber and vitamins you won't find in meat. Use whatever vegetables you like to make these savory pancakes—even leftovers from another recipe!

Ingredients

- 2 large eggs
- ½ tsp. salt
- ¾ c. all-purpose flour
- ½ c. ice water
- 1½ c. mixed vegetables such as zucchini, broccoli, bell peppers, green beans, or asparagus, *chopped very small*
- 2 green onions (scallions), *cut into 1-inch pieces*

Dipping Sauce:
- 2 tbsp. rice wine vinegar
- 2 tbsp. low-sodium soy sauce
- 1 tsp. sugar
- Pinch of red chile flakes, *or to taste*
- 2 tsp. vegetable oil

Directions

1. In a medium bowl, whisk eggs and salt until frothy. Add flour and ice water. Then, stir to make a thick batter. Gently stir in vegetables and green onions.
2. In a small skillet, heat half the oil over medium heat. Spoon in half the batter to make a pancake, spreading the vegetables evenly. Cook until crisp and golden, 4 to 5 minutes per side. Repeat with remaining oil and batter.
3. In a small bowl, stir together all ingredients for the dipping sauce.
4. Cut pancakes into quarters, arrange on a platter, and serve with dipping sauce.

✳ **Tip:** *Replace ½ c. of the vegetables with diced kimchi or chopped, cooked, shrimp.*

Nutrition Info *per 2-piece serving*

Total calories: 165
Carbohydrates: 22 g
Total fat: 5 g
Saturated fat: 1 g
Protein: 7.3 g
Fiber: 1.7 g
Sodium: 465 mg

💡 What ingredients could you add to this recipe to make it extra appealing?

When could you make or serve this dish?

What do you think the purpose of the eggs are in this recipe?

RECIPES AND MEAL PLANNING

MEATBALL SOUP

Ready In 40 min. **Serves** 8

Soups that include vegetables and lean meat are a great way to make hearty, economical one-pot meals. Use low-sodium stock when you can since packaged stock tends to be very salty. This recipe can be made with any lean ground meat you like; it gets lots of flavor from fresh herbs. Consider adding fresh chopped chiles, or chile powder, for added kick!

Ingredients

- 4 c. water
- 4 c. reduced-sodium chicken broth
- 2 lbs. ground lean turkey
- ¼ c. mint leaves, *finely chopped*
- 1 clove garlic, *minced*
- ¼ tbsp. ground black pepper
- 2 plum tomatoes, *diced*
- ½ c. fresh cilantro, *chopped*
- 1 large potato, *chopped*
- 2 carrots, *chopped*
- 1 celery stalk, *chopped*
- 2 zucchinis or yellow squash, *chopped*

Directions

1. In a pot, over medium heat: bring water and chicken broth to a boil.
2. While the liquids come to a boil, mix ground turkey, mint, garlic, pepper, and chopped tomato.
3. Roll the mixture into little balls, about 1-1½ inch diameter.
4. Once the liquids are boiling, add meatballs and cilantro. Lower heat and cook covered for 10 minutes.
5. When meatballs rise to the top, add potatoes, carrots, and celery. Continue to cook covered.
6. Once the vegetables are soft, add the zucchini and let it cook for 10 more minutes or until zucchini is tender before serving.

Tip: For added flavor, add lime juice, chopped chile pepper, or chopped onion to your bowl.

Nutrition Info *per 1½ cup serving*

Total calories: 203
Carbohydrates: 5 g
Total fat: 10 g
Saturated fat: 3 g
Protein: 18 g
Fiber: 2 g
Sodium: 348 mg

How would you adapt this recipe for your family?

What grain might you add to this soup?

What other meat, vegetable, and flavor combinations could you turn into a soup like this?

MU SHU VEGETABLES

Ready In 20 min. **Serves** 4

Very colorful foods are often more appealing to the eye than foods that are only one color. Eating a variety of colorful fruits and vegetables every day also helps to ensure you're getting the different vitamins you need. This colorful stir-fry is an Americanized version of a Chinese dish. It is usually eaten in a flour wrap, similar to a flour tortilla but you can also have it over rice.

Ingredients

- 2 tbsp. vegetable oil
- 1 piece (about 1-inch) fresh ginger, *peeled then grated or minced*
- 3 cloves garlic, *minced*
- 1 tbsp. toasted sesame oil
- 1 small cabbage, preferably Napa or Savoy, *very thinly sliced* (about 5-6 c.)
- 1 red bell pepper, *very thinly sliced*
- 3 medium carrots, *coarsely shredded* (about 2 c.)
- 1 tbsp. soy sauce
- 1 tbsp. cornstarch
- ¾ c. cold water
- 2 c. cooked rice or 4 warmed flour tortillas, preferably whole grain

Directions

1. In a large skillet, heat oil on medium-high heat. Add ginger and garlic and stir-fry for a few seconds.
2. Add the sesame oil, onion, and cabbage and stir-fry for two minutes. Add the peppers and carrots. Stir-fry for a little longer.
3. Add the soy sauce and stir-fry for another minute.
4. Stir the cornstarch into the water. Add to skillet and let simmer for two minutes or until liquid is thickened and evaporated.
5. Eat the vegetables rolled up in warmed flour tortillas or over rice.

Nutrition Info *per ¼ cup serving*

Total calories: 226
Carbohydrates: 28 g
Total fat: 11 g
Saturated fat: 1 g
Protein: 6 g
Fiber: 3 g
Sodium: 543 mg
Added Sugar: <1 g

What color fruit or vegetable is hardest for you to eat enough of?

Do you know anyone who eats mostly brown or white foods? Do you think they would try these Mu Shu Vegetables?

What other vegetables might you use in this dish?

NO-COOK CHOCOLATE PUDDING

Ready In 25 min. | **Serves** 6

Have a chocolate or a sweet tooth? This is a perfect recipe to provide a little chocolatey goodness as well as some healthy fats from avocados. Cocoa powder is made from crushed cocoa beans, the same beans used to make chocolate. Cocoa beans aren't naturally sweet--the sugar is added in the chocolate making process.

Ingredients

- 2 ripe avocados, *peeled and cubed*
- 1 banana, *peeled and cubed*
- ¼ c. cocoa powder unsweetened
- ¼ c. milk or non-dairy alternatives (almond or coconut are a good choice)
- 2 tablespoons honey
- 1 teaspoon vanilla extract

Directions

1. Mix all ingredients together in a blender or food processor until creamy and smooth. Adjust texture and flavor by adding more cocoa powder or milk.
2. Spoon into individual cups if you want to be fancy. Chill in the refrigerator for 20 minutes (or eat right away if you can't wait!).
3. Top with your favorite fruit or sprinkle some toasted nuts or coconut on top.

Nutrition Info *per ½ cup serving*

Total calories: 160
Carbohydrates: 18 g
Total fat: 11 g
Saturated fat: 2 g
Protein: 3 g
Fiber: 6 g
Sodium: 64 mg
Added Sugar: 6 g

Does anyone at your house make desserts from scratch?

Do you notice a difference between homemade and store bought desserts? Does your family prefer one over the other?

PEAR, GRAPE, AND CUCUMBER SALAD

Ready In 5 min. **Serves** 4

We often hear that it's important to drink water. A diet rich in fruits and vegetables also contains lots of water from the plants themselves. The ingredients in this salad are all hydrating. This makes it a great snack whenever you need to feel refreshed.

Ingredients

- 2 tsp. olive oil
- 2 tbsp. lime juice
- ⅛ tsp. salt
- 1 large cucumber, *diced (peel if waxed)*
- 1½ c. seedless red grapes, *sliced in half*
- 2 pears, *diced*

Directions

1. In a large bowl, whisk oil, lime juice, and salt.
2. Add grapes, cucumber, and pears and toss before serving.

✻ **Tip:** Sprinkle with ground chile powder for a little kick.

Nutrition Info *per 1 cup serving*

Total calories: 73
Carbohydrates: 16 g
Total fat: 2 g
Saturated fat: <1 g
Protein: <1 g
Fiber: 2 g
Sodium: 52 mg

💡 What are some other foods that have a lot of water in them?

Why might it be helpful to get water from the foods we eat?

What else would you add to this salad to change the flavor?

PITA PIZZA

Ready In 20 min.
Serves 4

Pizza can be a nutritious, balanced meal if it's made with good ingredients. This recipe uses whole wheat pita, but you can substitute any whole-wheat bread, bagel, or tortilla you'd like. Simply look for the word "whole" in the first item on the ingredients list. Then add plenty of fresh vegetables on top. You might also try chopping the vegetables small and mixing them in the sauce if you have picky eaters at home!

Ingredients

- 4 whole wheat pita bread
- 1 c. part-skim mozzarella cheese, *shredded*
- 1 c. low-sodium tomato or pizza sauce
- 1 c. vegetables, such as bell peppers, broccoli, mushrooms, olives, pineapple, onions, tomatoes, asparagus, and/or zucchini, *diced*

Directions

1. Preheat oven or toaster oven to 425°F. Line baking sheet with foil for easy cleanup.
2. Place the pitas on a baking sheet for assembly. Spread the tomato sauce on the pita leaving room for crust.
3. Sprinkle with cheese and add the toppings.
4. Cook pizzas in the oven for 5-8 minutes, or until cheese is melted.
5. Let cool for a minute before eating.

✱ **Tip:** Use leftover veggies to cut down on prep time. Sprinkle with dried oregano, basil or chili flakes for even more flavor.

Nutrition Info *per pita*

Total calories: 213
Carbohydrates: 32 g
Total fat: 6 g
Saturated fat: 3 g
Protein: 13 g
Fiber: 6 g
Sodium: 460 mg

💡 How many food groups does this pizza have?

How would you change this recipe if you made it at home?

What other foods can be balanced— or not— depending on how you make them?

POPCORN AND TOPPINGS

Ready In 10 min. **Serves** 5

Did you know popcorn is a whole grain? That means it has more fiber and nutrients than chips or other snacks. It's also easy and inexpensive to make on the stove! Kids love to watch the cooking process and listen to the kernels pop (from a safe distance). They also love to add their own toppings.

Ingredients

- ½ c. popcorn kernels
- 2 tbsp. oil
- ½ tsp. salt
- Assorted toppings, such as paprika, cayenne pepper, nutritional yeast, Parmesan cheese, dried herbs

Directions

1. Add vegetable oil to a large saucepan with a lid.
2. Add popcorn kernels, cover, and heat on medium. You will hear the kernels begin to pop after a few minutes.
3. Shake the pan frequently, holding the lid in place, to make sure all the kernels cook evenly without burning.
4. When you hear the popping slow down, remove from heat. Carefully open the lid.
5. Pour into a serving bowl and add desired toppings.

Nutrition Info *per 3 cup serving*

Total calories: 135
Carbohydrates: 18 g
Total fat: 6 g
Saturated fat: <1 g
Protein: 3 g
Fiber: 3 g
Sodium: 200 mg

Do you like the seasoning used in this recipe? What other seasoning might you try instead?

Have you ever made popcorn on the stove? Was it easier or harder than you expected?

SALSA FRESCA

Ready In 15 min. | **Serves** 4

Salsas are an easy way to brighten up any meal and add beneficial nutrients without tons of salt or sugar. Many kids won't even realize they're eating vegetables! Salsas can also be made with other fruits and vegetables besides tomatoes, such as mango, peach, watermelon, pear, corn, or cucumber. Experiment with this recipe using whatever is fresh and inexpensive at the store.

Ingredients

- 4 stems fresh cilantro, *chopped (stems included)*
- 1 small red onion, *chopped*
- 1 medium green bell pepper, *chopped*
- Hot sauce or fresh hot peppers, *to taste* (optional)
- 6 plum tomatoes
- 2 tbsp. red wine vinegar
- 1 lime, *juiced*
- 1 tbsp. ground cumin
- 1 tsp. olive oil
- Salt, *to taste*

Directions

1. Roughly chop the cilantro. Cut the onion and peppers into large pieces. Process in a blender until coarsely chopped.
2. Quarter the tomatoes. Add, along with remaining ingredients and pulse until the mixture is chopped into small pieces.
3. Serve immediately, or cover and chill for up to three days.

No-blender Directions

1. Chop everything finely with a knife.
2. Grate the tomatoes on the large holes of a grater (over a bowl so you catch the juices!).
3. Combine all the ingredients and serve immediately or cover/chill for up to three days.

Nutrition Info *per ½ cup serving*

Total calories: 58
Carbohydrates: 10 g
Total fat: 2 g
Saturated fat: <1 g
Protein: 2 g
Fiber: 3 g
Sodium: 12 mg

What are the different flavors that you can taste in this salsa?

What would you like to eat with this salsa?

What other ingredients might you add to this recipe to give it a twist?

SAUTÉED BANANAS

Ready In 10 min. **Serves** 3

Sautéing brings out the banana's sweetness and creates a delicious caramel like crust. This technique can be applied to all kinds of fruit. Lower the amount of sugar if you are making with sweeter fruits. This also makes a good topping for pancakes, yogurt or oatmeal.

Ingredients

- 3 bananas firm but ripe
- 1 tsp. unsalted butter
- 1½ tbsp brown sugar
- ½ tsp. cinnamon, *or adjust to taste*
- 1½ tsp. fresh squeezed lemon juice

Directions

1. Peel bananas and cut in quarters, first by cutting in half widthwise then lengthwise.
2. In a skillet, over low heat: add butter, brown sugar and cinnamon; stir until bubbly.
3. Add banana quarters, cut side down; sauté 1-2 minutes or until golden brown.
4. Turn over and sauté the other side, until golden brown.
5. Sprinkle with the lemon juice.
6. Serve warm; drizzle pan juice over bananas.

Nutrition Info *per banana*

Total calories: 157
Carbohydrates: 37 g
Total fat: 4 g
Saturated fat: 2 g
Protein: 1 g
Fiber: 3 g
Sodium: 6 mg

What are some other things you can do with ripe or overripe bananas?

How might family members help you with this recipe?

What does the lemon juice do for this recipe?

SESAME CHICKEN STIR-FRY

Ready In 25 min. | **Serves** 4

Restaurant meals often have far more salt, fat, and sugar than you would use at home. This Sesame Chicken with vegetables does have a little sugar for sweetness, but it also gets a lot of sweetness from fresh bell pepper and snow peas. For a vegetarian version, substitute cubes of firm tofu for the chicken and add them with the vegetables.

Ingredients

- 2 tsp. oil
- 1 lb. boneless, skinless chicken, *cut into strips*
- 2 c. snow peas or snap peas, *trimmed*
- 1 medium red bell pepper, *chopped*
- 1 medium green bell pepper, *chopped*
- 3 tbsp. low-sodium soy sauce
- 2 tbsp. water
- 1½ tsp packed brown sugar
- ¼ tsp. ground ginger
- 1 tbsp. toasted sesame seeds
- 2 green onions, *sliced*
- 2 c. cooked brown rice

Directions

1. Heat oil in large skillet. Add chicken; cook and stir-fry for 5-8 minutes or until chicken is fully cooked. Add snow peas and bell peppers; stir fry for 3 to 4 minutes more until vegetables are crisp-tender.
2. In a small bowl, combine soy sauce, water, brown sugar, and ginger; add to skillet. Cook for 3-5 minutes over medium-high heat.
3. Sprinkle with sesame seeds and green onions. Serve over brown rice.

Nutrition Info *per 1¼ cup serving*

Total calories: 313
Carbohydrates: 28 g
Total fat: 7 g
Saturated fat: 1 g
Protein: 30 g
Fiber: 5 g
Sodium: 470 mg

Which flavors stand out in this recipe?

What other vegetables would you like to try in this dish?

SPAGHETTI WITH MEAT SAUCE

Ready In 40 min. **Serves** 8

Choosing extra lean or lean ground meat keeps this recipe heart healthy. If you want to make it vegetarian, substitute chopped mushrooms. This sauce is great to keep in the freezer for a last minute meal.

Ingredients

- 1 tbsp. olive oil
- 1 onion, *finely chopped*
- 1 bell pepper, *finely chopped*
- 4 cloves garlic, *minced*
- 1 pound lean ground turkey
- 1 (6-ounce) can tomato paste
- 1 (28-ounce) can low-sodium diced tomatoes
- 2 tsp. dried oregano
- 2 tsp. dried basil
- 1 tsp. salt
- ½ tsp. black pepper
- 1 pound pasta, preferably whole wheat

Directions

1. Heat olive oil in a medium pot over medium heat.
2. Cook onion and bell pepper until softened.
3. Add turkey and garlic. Cook, stirring occasionally for 8–10 minutes until meat is no longer pink. Add tomato paste and cook for 2 minutes.
4. Stir in tomatoes with their juice, oregano, basil, salt, and ground black pepper. Bring to a boil and reduce heat. Cover and simmer for 15–20 minutes, stirring occasionally.
5. Meanwhile, cook pasta according to package directions; drain well.
6. Serve sauce over spaghetti.

Nutrition Info *per 1½ cup serving*

Total calories: 360
Carbohydrates: 54 g
Total fat: 9 g
Saturated fat: 2 g
Protein: 22 g
Fiber: 9 g
Sodium: 197 mg

Are there non-meat eaters in your family? How would you adapt this for them?

What are some other recipes you could make and keep in the freezer for a quick meal?

What would you serve with this to make it into a balanced meal?

SPICED TRAIL MIX

Ready In 10 min.
Serves 12

Add on to end of existing note: Healthy snacks, containing a little protein and/or healthy fat, are a great way to keep your energy and mood steady through the day.

Ingredients

- 1 c. peanuts or other nuts
- 1 c. raisins or other dried fruit
- 1 c. sunflower or pumpkin seeds, *raw or roasted*
- 1 c. bite-sized pretzels, dry low sugar cereal, or small crackers
- 1 tbsp. paprika and/or cinnamon
- Salt, *to taste*
- 1 c. dried shredded coconut, chocolate chips, or additional dried fruit (optional)

Directions

1. Toss all ingredients well and enjoy.

✻ **Tip:** Look for cereals with less than 6g of sugar per serving.

Nutrition Info *per ¼ cup serving*

Total calories: 196
Carbohydrates: 19 g
Total fat: 13 g
Saturated fat: 2 g
Protein: 6 g
Fiber: 4 g
Sodium: 113 mg

💡 What other ingredients might you use or substitute in this recipe?

Do you like the seasoning used in this recipe? What other seasoning might you try instead?

How might a snack like this come in handy in your life?

SPINACH AND CITRUS SALAD

Ready In 15 min. | **Serves** 4

If you have a sweet tooth, try adding naturally sweet ingredients to healthy dishes to satisfy your cravings. This salad gets plenty of sweetness from fresh orange segments and dried cranberries, as well from a dressing made with orange juice. Sliced nuts give it a satisfying crunch.

Ingredients

- 3 c. baby spinach leaves, *washed*
- 3 oranges, *peeled and broken into sections or sliced*
- 3 tbsp. sliced almonds
- ¼ c. dried cranberries
- 1 tbsp. olive oil
- 3 tbsp. orange juice, *squeezed from 1 orange*
- 2 tbsp. rice vinegar

Directions

1. In a serving bowl, combine spinach, oranges, and cranberries.
2. In a bowl, whisk together olive oil, orange juice, and rice vinegar for the dressing.
3. Toss salad with dressing. Sprinkle with almonds and serve.

Nutrition Info *per 1 cup serving*

Total calories: 150
Carbohydrates: 21 g
Total fat: 4 g
Saturated fat: <1 g
Protein: 3 g
Fiber: 4 g
Sodium: 20 mg

What could you substitute for oranges and cranberries if they weren't available?

How does your body feel after eating a salad like this?

Do you like having a "crunch" added to your salads or dishes? What are other ingredients that you may use to do this?

SPRING SPREAD

Ready In: 10 min. **Serves:** 4

This spread makes a great snack, sandwich filling, or dip. It's also way more nutritious than packaged dips and spreads thanks to several colors of fresh vegetables. Note that the smaller you chop or grate the vegetables, the more the flavors blend together— and might make it more enticing to picky eaters.

Ingredients

- 4 oz. low-fat cream cheese, *whipped or softened*
- ½ carrot, *grated*
- ½ red bell pepper, *finely diced*
- 2 green onions, *finely chopped*
- 1 tbsp. fresh herbs, *chopped* (see tip)
- 1 tsp. freshly squeezed lemon or lime juice

Serve with: whole grain crackers, tortillas, bagels, celery sticks, or cucumber slices

Directions

1. Mix all ingredients with a rubber spatula until creamy.
2. Use as a spread for breads, crackers, or on vegetables.

Tip: This is a great way to use up leftover herbs (such as dill, thyme, oregano, basil) and vegetables.

Nutrition Info *per 2 tbsp. serving*

Total calories: 61
Carbohydrates: 3 g
Total fat: 4 g
Saturated fat: 3 g
Protein: 2 g
Fiber: <1 g
Sodium: 106 mg

How would you adapt this recipe for your family?

What are some other nutritious snack foods you like to keep on hand?

THREE BEAN CHILI

Ready In 45 min.   **Serves** 6

It's not necessary for most of us to eat meat at every meal, or even every day. Protein builds bones, muscles, cartilage, skin, and blood, but it can be found in foods other than meat. To make a satisfying vegetarian entrée, choose a recipe with plenty of fresh vegetables, whole grains, beans, and/or legumes.

Ingredients

- 1 tbsp. vegetable oil
- 1 onion, *diced*
- 2 cloves garlic, *finely chopped*
- 2 zucchini or yellow summer squash, *diced* (fresh or frozen)
- 1 c. corn fresh, canned, or frozen
- 2 bell peppers, *diced*
- ½ tsp. black pepper
- ½ tsp. salt
- 1 tbsp. chili powder
- 1 tsp. ground cumin
- 1 (16-oz.) can low-sodium pinto beans, *drained and rinsed*
- 1 (16-oz.) can low-sodium black beans, *drained and rinsed*
- 1 (16-oz.) can low-sodium red kidney beans, *drained and rinsed*
- 2 (15-oz.) cans low-sodium diced tomatoes
- 1 tbsp. molasses (optional)

Directions

1. In a stockpot, heat vegetable oil over medium heat. Add onion and garlic then cook until soft, about 2 minutes. Add zucchini or squash, corn, and bell peppers then cook until soft, about 5 minutes. Stir in remaining ingredients and bring to a boil.
2. Reduce heat, cover, and simmer for 20 to 25 minutes, stirring occasionally.
3. Serve immediately or cool completely then store in the refrigerator or freezer.

Nutrition Info *per 1 cup serving*

Total calories: 370
Carbohydrates: 66 g
Total fat: 5 g
Saturated fat: 1 g
Protein: 20 g
Fiber: 19 g
Sodium: 580 mg

What are some other ways to add beans to your diet?

If you made this for your friends, would they miss having meat? Why or why not?

TURKEY APPLE SAUSAGE MUFFIN SANDWICHES

Ready In 30 min. **Serves** 6

Fast food meals can be loaded with salt, fat, and sugar. They may taste good, but they leave us feeling weighed down. These homemade turkey sausage sandwiches have plenty of the protein and fiber that we need without the extra processed ingredients. They're not just for breakfast.

Ingredients

Turkey Apple Sausage:
- 1 pound lean ground turkey
- 1 red apple, *cored and finely chopped*
- 2 garlic cloves, *minced and divided*
- ½ tsp. dried thyme
- ¼ tsp. red pepper flakes
- 1 tsp. dried sage
- ¼ tsp. ground black pepper
- ⅛ tsp. ground coriander
- 2 tsp. oil

Breakfast Sandwich:
- 2 c. mushrooms, *chopped*
- 1 medium onion, *chopped*
- 6 whole wheat English muffins
- 6 slices tomato

Directions

1. In a large bowl, combine turkey, apple, one garlic clove, thyme, red pepper flakes, sage, ground black pepper, and coriander; mix well.
2. Form the turkey mixture into 6 patties.
3. Heat 1 tsp. oil in skillet over medium heat.
4. Cook patties until they are cooked through, about 5 to 7 minutes per side. Set aside.
5. Heat 1 tsp. oil in skillet over medium heat.
6. Add mushrooms, onions, and garlic. Sauté until the mushrooms are tender and onions begin to brown, about 5 minutes.
7. Cut each English muffin in half. Place a Turkey Apple Sausage patty, ⅙th of mushroom-onion mixture, and a slice of tomato on 6 English muffin halves.
8. Cover each sandwich with the other English muffin half and enjoy!

Nutrition Info *per muffin*

Total calories: 256   **Total fat:** 5 g   **Protein:** 19 g   **Sodium:** 459 mg
Carbohydrates: 35 g   **Saturated fat:** 1 g   **Fiber:** 6 g

How are these different in flavor, texture, and color than a fast food sandwich?

What ingredients would you add to this recipe? Take away?

What benefits do you think there are to using a whole wheat English muffin as opposed to a regular one?

UN-FRIED RICE

Ready In 30 min. **Serves** 4

To eat a balanced diet, it's not necessary to make several different dishes at each meal. Many easy, filling one-pot recipes include everything you need for a balanced meal. This recipe for "un-fried" rice is lower in fat and sodium than restaurant fried rice, and it contains at least three of the five food groups. This recipe comes out best with leftover rather than freshly cooked rice.

Ingredients

- 1 tbsp. oil
- 1 clove garlic, *minced*
- 2 c. diced raw vegetables such as onion, celery, bell pepper, cabbage, broccoli, green beans, peas, zucchini, mushrooms, or bean sprouts
- 1 egg, *beaten*
- 2 c. cooked rice cold, preferably brown rice
- 2 tbsp. low-sodium soy sauce
- Black pepper to taste
- 1 c. cooked chicken or shrimp (optional)
- 1 c. mango or pineapple, *chopped* (optional)

Directions

1. Heat oil until sizzling in the bottom of large skillet.
2. Stir-fry garlic and vegetables so they are cooked but still a little crisp.
3. Add shrimp or chicken to the skillet, if using, and cook for 2 minutes.
4. Push everything to one side. Add the egg directly into the exposed bottom of the pan and scramble.
5. Add rice, soy sauce, black pepper, and other optional ingredients. Turn heat down to medium-low. Cook until heated through, stirring frequently.

Nutrition Info *per 1 cup serving*

Total calories: 322
Carbohydrates: 50 g
Total fat: 9 g
Saturated fat: 1 g
Protein: 12 g
Fiber: 6 g
Sodium: 578 mg

How would you adapt this recipe for your family?

What do you think of adding the optional mango or pineapple to this dish? Do you like the combination of sweet and salty flavors in an entree?

Are there vegetarian proteins you might add to this dish?

VEGETABLE NOODLE BOWL

Ready In 20 min. **Serves** 8

Whole grain breads and pastas are often more filling than ones made from white flours because they have more fiber and healthy fats. They may also keep their texture longer without getting soggy. This recipe calls for whole wheat noodles. The longer the noodles sit, the more they absorb the seasonings in the recipe. Their hearty texture, when combined with crunchy vegetables, really gives you something to chew on!

Ingredients

- 1 pound whole wheat spaghetti (or any Asian noodles, like soba)
- 3 tbsp. low-sodium soy sauce
- 4 tsp. toasted sesame oil
- 1 tsp. hot chili sauce (like Sriracha), *to taste*
- 2 garlic cloves, *finely minced or grated*
- 1 bunch scallions, *chopped* (about 1 c.)
- 1 cucumber, *cut in half lengthwise and thinly chopped* (about 1 c.)
- 2 carrots, *coarsely grated* (about 1 c.)
- ½ head of cabbage, *shredded* (about 1 c.)
- Salt and pepper, *to taste*
- 1 c. firm tofu, *diced* (optional)

Directions

1. Prepare the noodles according to the package instructions. Rinse them under cold water and put them in a strainer to drain.
2. In a large bowl, mix the soy sauce, sesame oil, chili sauce, scallions, garlic, cucumber, carrot, and cabbage. Add the noodles toss everything together with a fork or tongs. Gently stir in tofu, if using. Taste and add salt and pepper as needed.
3. Let the noodles sit in the fridge for about an hour, if you can, before serving. The flavors will mingle and become more intense.

Nutrition Info *per 2 cup serving*

Total calories: 237
Carbohydrates: 45 g
Total fat: 4 g
Saturated fat: 1 g
Protein: 9 g
Fiber: 6 g
Sodium: 238 mg

What ingredients do you have at home that you can turn into a noodle bowl like this?

Does your family try to eat less meat? Why or Why not?

VEGETARIAN SUSHI ROLL

Ready In 60 min.   **Serves** 4

Brown rice is a good alternative to white rice as it includes fiber, which helps keep everything moving through our bodies. The bran content is also rich in B-complex vitamins and minerals, which helps us stay energized throughout the day. If family members are skeptical about it, try mixing brown and white rice in increasing proportions to get them used to the flavor and texture. Or introduce it with a fun recipe like this one that the whole family can prepare.

Ingredients

- 1 c. short grain brown rice
- 2 c. water
- 3 tbsp. rice vinegar
- 1 tsp. sugar
- 1 cup baby spinach leaves or alfalfa sprouts
- 1 cucumber
- 1 carrot
- 1 avocado
- 4 sheets nori (dried seaweed)
- Sesame seeds for garnish (optional)
- Low-sodium soy sauce for dipping

Directions

1. Rinse and drain brown rice, place into a saucepan over medium heat, and pour in water. Bring to a boil, and simmer until rice has absorbed the water, about 45 minutes. Add rice vinegar and sugar to cooked brown rice. Mix well and set aside.
2. Cut carrot and cucumber into 8 long thin strips, each. Cut seeds off cucumber strips.
3. Cut avocado into half, remove skin and pit; cut each half into 8 slices.
4. Place nori sheet horizontally in front of you. Spread rice evenly on 2/3 of nori sheet; lay a few leaves of spinach or a small amount of sprouts in the bottom third of the rice. Place 2 cucumber strips, 2 carrot strips, and 4 pieces avocado on top. (*One possible layout is shown right.*)
5. Slightly dampen the top edge of the nori. Starting from the bottom, roll up tightly. Press the damp edge to seal.
6. Cut into thick pieces and sprinkle with sesame seeds, if desired. Enjoy with or without soy sauce.

*❋ **Tip:** Three cups leftover cooked rice can be used in this recipe. Slightly warm it before adding the vinegar and sugar. Make sure your hands are dry before rolling your sushi.*

Nutrition Info *per roll*

Total calories: 279
Carbohydrates: 50 g
Total fat: 9 g
Saturated fat: 1 g
Protein: 6 g
Fiber: 6 g
Sodium: 47 mg

💡 Do your family members enjoy finger foods like this?

What are some other healthy finger foods your family enjoys?

VEGGIE SCRAMBLE

Ready In 7 min. | **Serves** 4

Many of us are too rushed in the morning to cook a big breakfast. We may end up eating sugary processed food, fast food, or nothing at all! This can affect our moods and energy throughout the day. Fortunately, scrambled eggs are quick and inexpensive. When prepared with vegetables—even frozen vegetables—they are more nutritious and filling.

Ingredients

- 8 tsp. olive oil
- 8 eggs
- 1⅓ c. fresh or frozen veggies, *chopped* (such as spinach, kale, chard, peppers, peas, onion, summer squash, mushrooms)
- Salt, *to taste*
- Pepper, *to taste*

Directions

1. Sauté veggies in a medium skillet with 1 tsp. of olive oil. Place in a medium-size bowl.
2. Add 1 tsp. olive oil to skillet, add eggs and stir over medium heat.
3. When eggs are partially cooked, add sautéed veggies. Cook until eggs are just set. Add a pinch of salt, pepper, and desired toppings.

❋ **Tip:** Serve over brown rice or in a warmed whole wheat tortilla or pita bread for a complete meal.

Nutrition Info *per 1 cup serving*

Total calories: 225
Carbohydrates: 1 g
Total fat: 18.5 g
Saturated fat: 3 g
Protein: 13 g
Fiber: <1 g
Sodium: 150 mg

💡 Do you think a veggie scramble could keep you full for longer than a donut or bagel? Why?

What seasonings or condiments would you use to add flavor?

WHOLE WHEAT PANCAKE

Ready In 25 min. **Serves** 4

Who needs pancake mix? Making pancakes from scratch is almost as fast and cheaper. Using whole grain flours also makes it healthier and more filling. This Whole Wheat Pancake holds up to all kinds of toppings without getting mushy like white pancakes. It can also made on a stove top or in a rice cooker!

Ingredients

- 1 c. whole wheat flour
- 2 tsp. baking powder
- ¼ tsp. salt
- 1 egg
- 1 c. milk or non-dairy alternatives
- 1 tbsp. canola oil or melted butter (optional)
- 1 c. sliced banana, chopped apple or berries (fresh or frozen) (optional)
- Oil or butter for greasing the pan

Stove Top Directions

1. Heat wide skillet over medium heat.
2. In a bowl, mix together dry ingredients.
3. In a separate bowl, whisk eggs, milk, and melted butter or oil, if using. Add to flour mixture and stir.
4. Grease the pan with a little oil or butter. Spoon ¼ c. batter into the hot skillet.
5. Once pancake is bubbling and dry around the edges, flip it.
6. Cook for about 3 minutes more, or until the center of the pancake is completely dry.
7. Repeat until the batter is finished. Top with fruit, if using, and serve.

Rice Cooker Directions

1. Grease a rice cooker with butter or oil.
2. Mix other ingredients well in a bowl.
3. Pour batter into the rice cooker.
4. Cook for 1–2 cycles, or until the cake is dry in the middle.
5. Remove dish from rice cooker and flip it onto a plate. The pancake should pop out.
6. Slice the pancake in 4 and serve with your favorite topping.

Nutrition Info *per ¼-piece serving*

Total calories: 217   **Total fat:** 7 g   **Protein:** 8 g   **Sodium:** 293 mg
Carbohydrates: 34 g   **Saturated fat:** 2 g   **Fiber:** 5 g

What is the benefit of mixing the dry ingredients and liquid ingredients separately before combining?

Why does whole grain flour have a stronger taste than white flour?

What other toppings would taste good with this pancake?

YOGURT PARFAIT

Ready In 15 min. **Serves** 4

Looking at labels when shopping for ingredients can make all the difference of whether a dish is healthy or not. This recipe is a good example. When made with unsweetened yogurt, fresh fruit, and lower-sugar cereal, the parfait makes a nutritious breakfast or snack. When made with sweetened yogurt and cereal however, it may contain more added sugar than a candy bar! Check "Added Sugars" on the Nutrition Facts labels to find products with few or no added sugars.

Ingredients

- 2 c. fresh fruit or frozen fruit, try at least two different kinds, *chopped*
- 2 c. unsweetened yogurt
- 2 tbsp. 100% fruit spread or honey
- 1 c. low sugar granola or low sugar dry cereal

Directions

1. Wash and cut fruit into small pieces.
2. In a bowl, mix the yogurt and fruit spread together.
3. Layer each of the parfaits in four bowls, mugs, or glasses as follows: ¼ c. fruit, ¼ c. yogurt, 2 tbsp. granola (repeat one more time). Do this for all four servings.

✻ *Tip: Use a clear glass/plastic cup or jar when you make these so you can see the beautiful layers.*

Nutrition Info *per 1 cup serving*

Total calories: 272
Carbohydrates: 44 g
Total fat: 7 g
Saturated fat: 4 g
Protein: 9 g
Fiber: 4 g
Sodium: 137 mg

What other foods does your family eat that might have added sugars?

If you are trying to reduce your family's sugar consumption, what might be some ways to do it?

WRITE YOUR OWN RECIPE: OVEN-BAKED OMELETTE (A.K.A. FRITTATA)

■ _____'s _____ and _____ Oven-baked Omelette
   name someone special   *vegetable*   *another vegetable*

Serves: 6

1. Preheat the oven to 350°F.

2. In a big bowl, whisk 8 eggs with ½ cup of _____.
   milk or non-dairy alternative

3. Heat 2 tablespoons of butter or oil in a large oven-proof skillet over medium heat.

   Then add 1–2 cups of chopped _____.
   your chosen vegetables

4. When the vegetables are tender, add 1 teaspoon _____.
   dried herbs or spices

5. Pour the egg mixture over top the other ingredients in the skillet. Allow to cook, without stirring, for 1–2 minutes.

6. Sprinkle with a handful of crumbled _____, if desired, then bake in the oven
   cheese

   for 15–20 minutes or until the center is just firm.

7. Remove the frittata from the oven and let cool a little before slicing and serving.

❋ *Tip: If you don't have an oven-proof skillet, oil or butter the bottom of a baking pan. Spread vegetable mixture on the bottom and pour in beaten eggs before baking.*

IDEA BANK

Vegetables
spinach
squash
mushrooms
Swiss chard
asparagus
peas
corn kernels
onion
broccoli
bell pepper

Herbs and Spices
basil
oregano
thyme
parsley
tarragon
chile powder
turmeric
cilantro

Cheese
Parmesan or Romano
cheddar
mozzarella
Swiss cheese
Jack cheese

WRITE YOUR OWN RECIPE: CHEESY BAKED PASTA

■ Cheesy Baked _____ with _____
           pasta   *one selected ingredient or seasoning from the recipe*

Serves: 8

1. Preheat oven to 400°F. Grease a baking dish.

2. Boil a large pot of salted water. Add 1 pound of whole grain _____
   pasta
   and cook until it's almost, but not quite, done (still a little firm, also known as *al dente*).

3. While the pasta cooks, grate 8 oz. _____ into a large bowl.
   cheese
   Add a cup of milk and a teaspoon of _____.
   herbs and spices

4. Fold in 2 cups of chopped _____ and some _____.
   greens   *extras*

5. If you'd like, sprinkle some _____ over the top.
   toppings

6. Drain the pasta and mix with the other ingredients. Then pour the whole thing into your baking dish.
   Bake 15 minutes or until golden brown on top.

IDEA BANK

Pasta
macaroni (or whole wheat macaroni)
spaghetti
shells
penne
rice stick noodles
egg noodles

Cheese
Parmesan
cheddar
Monterey Jack cheese
Gruyère, mozzarella, or Swiss

Herbs and Spices
dried or fresh oregano
fresh basil
fresh parsley
chile powder
garlic powder
mustard

Greens (raw or cooked)
cooked spinach
Swiss chard
kale
arugula
collards

Extras
cooked chicken, ham, or sausage
caramelized onions
sautéed mushrooms
chopped sun-dried tomatoes
chopped pitted olives
corn
frozen peas
cooked broccoli or cauliflower

Toppings
bread crumbs or croutons
crispy onions
crushed crackers or chips
more shredded cheese

WRITE YOUR OWN RECIPE: DINNER SALAD

■ _____'s Dinner Salad with _____ and _____
   name someone special   *salad greens*   *protein or whole grain*

Serves: 6

1. In a giant bowl, whisk together ⅓ cup olive oil with 3 tablespoons _____,
   acid

   1 teaspoon _____, and a pinch of salt.
   dried spices or herbs

2. To the bowl, add up to 2 cups each of _____, _____,
   crunchy raw vegetables   *your chosen cooked protein or whole grain*

   _____, and _____. Toss them in the dressing. Taste a piece of
   something juicy, chopped   *another fruit or vegetable*

   lettuce and adjust seasonings or acid.

3. Add about 6 cups of _____, chopped or torn in bite-sized pieces.
   your chosen salad greens

4. Add up to 1 cup of _____.
   something with texture, for fun

5. Toss everything really well to coat with the dressing. Serve at room temperature.

IDEA BANK

Acids
fresh citrus juice
apple cider
balsamic vinegar
wine vinegar
rice vinegar with a little soy sauce
Or try a combination!

Herbs and Spices
basil
oregano
thyme
parsley
mint
ginger
chile flakes
mustard
black pepper

Raw Vegetables
chopped bell peppers
chopped or shredded carrots
sliced avocado
sliced cucumbers
chopped celery
shaved fennel

Cooked Proteins & Whole Grains
cooked chicken, turkey, or steak
cooked shrimp
canned tuna or salmon (drained)
cubed marinated tofu
sliced hard-boiled egg
cooked whole legumes like chickpeas or kidney beans
cooked quinoa
cooked whole grain pasta
cooked wild rice, brown rice, or red rice

Something Juicy
tomatoes
corn kernels
orange or grapefruit segments
sliced plums or peaches
sliced apples or pears
chunks of mango or pineapple

Salad Greens
spinach
lettuce
cabbage
arugula
kale
Or try a combination!

Fun additions
pitted olives
nuts or seeds
crumbled or shredded salty cheese
sliced soft cheese
crunchy tortilla strips or croutons
dried fruit such as raisins, cranberries, cherries
Or try a combination!

WRITE YOUR OWN RECIPE: FRIED "RICE"

■ Fried _____ with _____ and _____
       whole grain   *protein*   *vegetable or fruit*

Serves: 4 *(If doubling this recipe, make in batches or use two pans.)*

1. Heat a big skillet over high heat, then add 2 tablespoons vegetable oil (not olive).

2. When the oil is hot, turn down the heat to medium, and add a handful of chopped _____.
   type of onion, garlic, or shallot

3. Stir in a cup of _____.
   your chosen protein

4. When the protein is cooked through, remove from pan and set aside. Add 1 tbsp. vegetable oil and 2 cups chopped _____. Keep stirring.
   vegetables, at least 2 kinds

5. Add 2 cups of cold cooked _____, ½ cup of _____,
   your chosen whole grain   *something fun (optional)*
   and a few tablespoons of _____.
   salty or spicy sauce

6. Stir everything until all the ingredients are heated through and steaming. Taste and adjust the seasonings. Serve hot.

IDEA BANK

Proteins
peeled shrimp
chopped chicken breast
chopped ham
lean ground beef or turkey
cubed tofu, tempeh, or seitan
eggs, beaten

Whole Grains
brown rice
quinoa
barley
farro
whole wheat couscous

Vegetables
celery
zucchini
carrots
peas
bell peppers
broccoli or cauliflower
scallions
mushrooms
cabbage
asparagus
green beans

Fun Additions
roasted peanuts, walnuts, or cashews
chopped mango or pineapple
sesame seeds

Salty or Spicy Sauces
soy sauce
teriyaki sauce
fish sauce
sweet chile sauce
hot sauce

RECIPE TEMPLATE

■ _____
    short, but descriptive and appealing, recipe title

Yield: 4-6 servings

Ingredients

_____
_____
_____
_____
_____
_____
_____
_____

Include at least one or two fruits and/or vegetables. Don't forget amounts and prep details (chopped, cooked, etc.).

Add whole grains, protein foods, dairy, or all three.

Remember the seasonings, salt, herbs, spices, or sauces.

Directions

1. First, _____
   _____

2. Next, _____
   _____

3. Then, _____
   _____

4. Finally, _____
   _____

5. Serve with _____

   Don't forget to _____!

If the recipe is cooked, give instructions for heating the stove, oven, or other appliance.

Remember to describe what equipment to use.

How will people know when each step is complete or the recipe is finished? Give sensory details.

EATFRESH.ORG

Where do you find trustworthy nutrition information online?

EatFresh.org makes shopping and home cooking easy. Go to EatFresh.org right now and start exploring!

» Find healthy, inexpensive, and quick recipes, including those found in this workbook.
» Print, save, share, and text recipes to your mobile phone.
» Learn lifestyle tips to keep you healthy and feeling your best.
» Ask a registered dietitian a question about nutrition, cooking, or healthy eating.
» Save time planning and shopping with meal plans.
» Apply for CalFresh/SNAP.
» Learn basic cooking skills and how to substitute ingredients to use what you already have at home.
» View the website in English, Spanish, or Chinese.
» View nutrition information for each recipe.

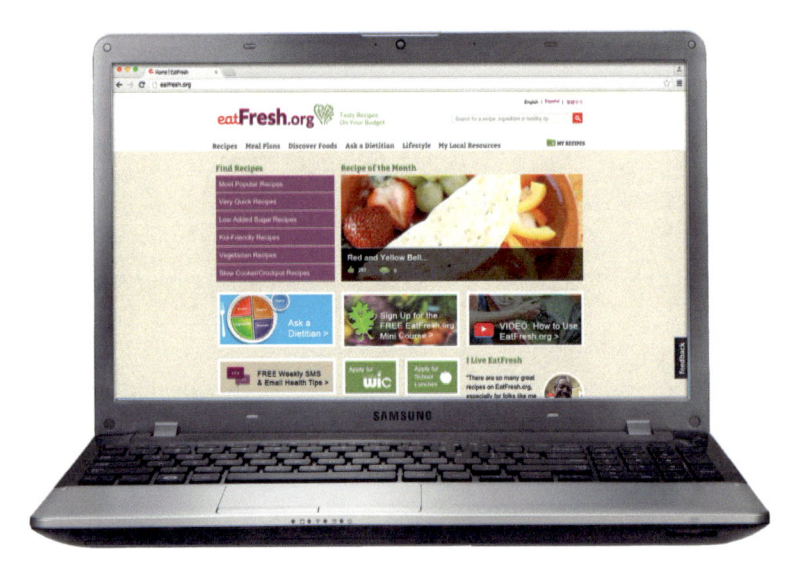

MINDFULNESS ACTIVITIES

SOUP BOWL BREATHING

When you need to clear your mind, de-stress, get focused, or wind down, try this 90 second exercise.

Think of your favorite soup.

Gently cup your hands like you are holding your favorite soup. You can also just put your hands down in your lap. Sit up tall, like your spine was made of a stack of pennies, with both feet on the floor. Close your eyes or glance down.

Imagine breathing in like you are smelling a delicious bowl of soup, and breathing out like you are blowing on it to cool down—carefully so as not to splash soup everywhere!

Breathe in for four seconds.

Breathe out for eight seconds.

Repeat three times.

Do you need a ritual to connect with your mind, body, or spirit? Try this one whenever you need it.

Put your feet flat on the ground.

Silently, to yourself, name **five things you can see** in the room...

Now name **four things you can hear** in the room...

Next, name **three sensations you feel in your body**...

Then, name **two things you can smell**...

And finally, [*pick one thing to consider from the list below*]

> ...one thing for which you are grateful.
>
> ...one thing that inspires you.
>
> ...one person you appreciate.
>
> ...one wish for the world.
>
> ...one hope or dream for yourself.
>
> ...one good quality about yourself.

SELF HOLDING

Self holding uses the sense of touch to help the nervous system more easily calm down during times of stress or agitation.

Like other mindfulness techniques, this could help you to be present, focused and more relaxed when you are feeling overwhelmed or stuck. You can even do this when you need to fall asleep. You can also teach this to your children or do it to them so that they can calm their bodies and minds.

1. Get into a comfortable position either seated or lying down.

2. Place one hand on your forehead. Place the other hand on your heart.

3. Gently place your attention on the area between your two hands, the area inside yourself between your head and heart.

4. Just feel what goes on in the area between your hands. Gently breathe in and out.

5. Do this for as long as you can or need to in order to feel yourself shift into a more relaxed state.

MINDFUL EATING

Mindful eating helps us nourish our mind and body. Use these reminders to help take care of yourself when you eat.

☑ *Learn your hunger cues*—Are you actually hungry or are you instead tired, stressed out, bored, or thirsty?

☑ *Avoid overeating*—Pay attention to your portion size. Slow down as the meal progresses, notice when you are full, and decide if you want to stop eating.

☑ *Pay attention to how you eat*—Take time to taste and enjoy your food. Try not to multitask or use a screen while eating.

☑ *Nourish your mind and body*—Pay attention to what you eat. Food affects how well your mind and body functions.

Made in the USA
Columbia, SC
22 April 2024